The Medieval Churches of the City of Norwich

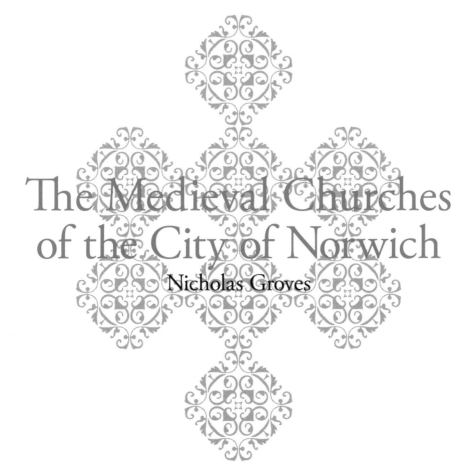

The Medieval Churches
of the City of Norwich

Nicholas Groves

The Medieval Churches
of the City of Norwich

Published by Norwich Heritage Economic
and Regeneration Trust (HEART) and
East Publishing Limited.

Norwich HEART
PO Box 3130
Norwich NR2 1XR
www.heritagecity.org

Norwich HEART is a private, charitable
company set up to act as an umbrella
organisation for all the city's heritage.
We strategically plan, regenerate, manage
and promote Norwich's heritage and act
as a best practice exemplar nationally and
internationally for developing heritage as a
vehicle for social and economic regeneration.

East Publishing Limited
9 Rigby's Court
Norwich NR2 1NT
www.eastpublishing.com

Text © Nicholas Groves 2010

Vox pops by Christina Lister.
Edited, designed and brought to production by
East Publishing.

ISBN 978-0-9560385-1-7 (paperback)

ISBN 978-0-9560385-2-4 (hardback)

Printed and bound in Great Britain by
the MPG Books Group, Bodmin and
King's Lynn.

Every reasonable effort has been made to
establish the copyright holders of all the
photographs used in this book. Any errors or
omissions are inadvertent. Anyone who has
not been contacted is invited to write to the
publisher so that a proper acknowledgement
can be included in subsequent editions of
this book.

Front cover: flint work, St Andrews; detail
of east window, St Peter Mancroft; detail of
wooden font cover, St Peter Mancroft

Page 8: interior and reflections, St Stephen's

Pages 148–149: view to the north from the
City Hall tower

Page 158: bench end, St Helen's (see also
page 55)

Back cover: detail of medieval font,
St Julian's (originally from All Saints)

Photography credits, subject specified where
more than one person's work appears on a page:

Norfolk Library and Information Service
– to view thousands of images of Norfolk's
history visit www.picture.norfolk.gov.uk
31 (exterior), 68, 72, 77, 78 (postcard),
82 (exterior), 85, 113, 124 (postcard) 131, 140
(tower)

Norfolk Museums & Archaeology Service
(Norwich Castle Museum & Art Gallery) 23,
26, 37, 40, 47 (brass), 52, 65, 80, 92, 101, 105
(drawing), 108, 114 (drawing), 118, 123, 126,
134, 141 (drawing), 143 (screen), 144 (drawing)

Norwich HEART 16 (memorial slab), 21 (flint
galletting and coats of arms), 24 (exterior), 63
(clerestory), 139 (remains)

Norwich Arts Centre 135 (interior)

East Publishing front cover (flint work and font
cover), 47 (lectern), 51 (painting), 74 (font), 79
(spandrel), 84, 93, 98 (tower), 99 (door), 103
(interior)

Ricky-Joe Burrage 53, 54 (interior), 55

Sophie Cabot 139 (monuments)

Rachel Codling 106 (slab), 107 (tower, clock
and statue)

Mike Dixon 103 (window), 109

Ian 'Harry' Harris 76, 99 (interior and
tympanum), 129 (tower)

Simon Knott 14, 17 (window), 24 (screen), 27
(brass), 29 (nave), 35, 42 (window), 51 (exterior),
56 (window), 59 (interior and auditorium),
62 (window), 67 (window), 74 (doorway and
interior), 75 (statue), 78 (stained glass), 106 (glass),
117 (interior), 132 (window), 137 (new lobby)

David Plummer 111 (glass detail)

George and Jonathan Plunkett 16 (font), 17, 19,
20 (monument), 25, 28, 29 (font and exterior),
31 (interior), 32, 34 (font and exterior), 38
(tomb), 43 (interior), 46 (bells), 57, 58 (font
and interior), 62 (interior), 63 (exterior), 66
(interior), 67 (exterior), 69, 70 (font and porch),
71 (interior), 74 (interior and exterior), 78
(interior), 82 (interior and font), 86, 88, 90
(interior and tomb), 94 (interior and exterior),
96, 97, 102 (interior and door), 105 (interior),
106 (font), 110 (font and door), 120 (interior and
monument), 124, 128 (interiors and exterior),

136, 137 (exterior), 139 (ruins), 140 (exterior
and interior), 141 (stone corbel), 142, 143
(exterior and interior)

Leo Reynolds 24 (glass detail), 50 (glass detail),
58 (carved support), 59 (tower), 63 (ceiling
detail and porch), 66 (statue and organ detail),
81, 87 (monument), 89, 90 (wall text), 91 (glass
and slab details), 112, 117 (statue), 125 (glass
details), 132 (misericord), 133 (exterior)

Marion Ridgley 54 (window)

John Sapey 144 (exterior)

Cameron Self 16 (exterior), 27 (exterior), 31
(exterior), 33, 56 (exterior), 91 (exterior), 98
(porch), 110 (exterior), 119, 120 (exterior), 125
(exterior), 127

Chris Skipworth 15, 21(exterior), 22, 36, 45, 50
(exterior), 60, 64, 79 (exterior), 83 (interior), 95
(exterior), 100, 102 (interior), 114 (tower), 122,
128 (east window), 135 (exterior)

Richard Tilbrook (courtesy of Norfolk Library
and Information Service, and Roy Tricker) 68,
82 (exterior), 140 (tower)

EM Trendell (www.norwich-churches.org) 70
(reredos)

Seany 1968 16 (interior), 24 (window), 67
(interior), 71 (exterior), 75 (tower), 87 (interiors),
94 (roof), 95 (interior), 121 (interior), 133
(interior), 138, 144 (remains)

Emma Whitcombe 18, 20 (stalls and monument
detail), 21 (monuments), 46 (exterior), 107
(porch), 121 (reredos)

Photographers who submitted images to
the 2009 Norwich HEART photography
competition on Norwich's medieval churches:

Jan Barsby 132 (nave)

Joan Blazeby 137 (interior)

Julia Cameron 8, 114 (transept), 115 (monument)

Ian Coldicott 117 (quire stalls)

David Drinkwater 34 (door)

David Edleston front cover (window), 41, 66
(rood figures), 111 (benches), 116

Raymond Gouldsmith 27 (clock), 42
(monument), 104 (interior), 111 (interior)

George Ishmael 54 (exterior), 104 (tower)

Helen Litterick 50 (interior), 78 (interior), 158

Tracy Martin 42 (exterior)

Sheena McIntyre-Warnock 43 (statue), 130

Gary Rayner 83 (interior)

David Sherwood 47 (play area), 115 (interior)

Jeffrey Taylor 44, 48, 148

Paul Venn 38 (exterior)

David White 39, 73

Contents

The author   6
Foreword by Professor Paul Binski   7
A remarkable ecclesiastical set,
by Michael Loveday, Chief Executive,
Norwich HEART   9
About this book, by Nicholas Groves   10
Introduction   11

All Saints   14
St Andrew   18
St Augustine   22
St Clement-at-Fyebridge   26
St Edmund   30
St Etheldreda   32
St George Colegate   36
St George Tombland   40
St Giles-on-the-Hill   44
St Gregory   48
St Helen   52
St James Pockthorpe   56
St John Maddermarket   60
St John Timberhill   64
St John-de-Sepulchre   68
St Julian   72
St Lawrence   76
St Margaret-de-Westwick   80
St Martin-at-Oak   84

St Martin-at-Palace   88
St Mary Coslany   92
St Mary-the-Less   96
St Michael Coslany (St Miles)   100
St Michael-at-Plea   104
St Peter Hungate   108
St Peter Mancroft   112
St Peter Parmentergate   118
St Saviour   122
St Simon and St Jude   126
St Stephen   130
St Swithin   134

Lost churches   138
St Bartholomew   139
St Benedict   140
St Crowches   141
St Michael-at-Thorn   142
St Paul   143
St Peter Southgate   144
Churches lost before 1600   145

Glossary   150
Bibliography   152
Acknowledgements   153
Index   154
Map and accessibility information   156

The author Nicholas Groves is a native of
Norfolk, and has always been interested in all
aspects of church history and archaeology. He has
a long-standing association with the churches of
Norwich, serving as organist at St Julian's, 1981–92,
and St George Tombland, 1989–2006, where he still
acts as parish archivist. His doctoral research was on
Anglican Ritualism in 19th-century Norwich, and
in 2005 he was appointed a trustee of the Norwich
Historic Churches Trust. He is also a fellow of
the Royal Historical Society, and a member of the
Ecclesiastical History Society.

He has taught in Norfolk since 1979, both
in schools and in higher education. His other
publications include works on Sarah Glover, the
originator of the tonic sol-fa system of musical
notation; on the history of theological training in
the Church of England; and on the life and work
of St Fursa, the seventh-century Irish missionary
who worked in Norfolk.

Foreword

Paul Binski, Professor of the History of Medieval Art,
Cambridge University

The place of churches of all sorts in the urban and rural landscape of Britain has never been more important. We now see these wonderful buildings as works of art and documents of history, as well as places where, as the poet T S Eliot put it, "prayer has been valid". In Norwich, a city almost unique in Europe in the amazing density of its churches and number of survivals relative to its size, many of these buildings continue to function as centres of worship too. To make sure that all the churches survive and flourish, one thing is especially important: that people should get to know them in an accessible way. Using churches is one of the best ways of preserving them. The work of the Norwich Historic Churches Trust is devoted to this task of education and support, helping the specialist, the enthusiast, or just anyone wandering through Norwich's lanes.

Churches can be known in all sorts of ways – as familiar local landmarks, rather like our local pubs; as places to which a family's history is tied; or as striking galleries of works of art which would grace a museum or art gallery. Norwich's churches possess wonderful furniture, brilliant stained glass, all sorts of tombs, space and atmosphere. The names alone – St John Maddermarket, St Peter Parmentergate and so on – are romantic enough. Only London can compete, but Norwich retains far more of its medieval past. That so much has survived, whether in grand St Peter Mancroft or cosy St Peter Hungate, is a miracle. Equally important buildings reflect Norwich's post-Reformation history and tradition of non-conformity. Every few yards something catches the eye.

I cannot think of a better guide to all Norwich's churches than Nicholas Groves. This book is a splendid celebration of our fine city's proud heritage.

A remarkable ecclesiastical set

Michael Loveday, Chief Executive, Norwich HEART

"I saw with pleasure and surprise, the beautious tow'rs of Norwich...
No situation can it surpass in any nation" Alexander Geddes, 1742

In 2008, when Norwich Heritage Economic & Regeneration Trust
(HEART) decided to produce a publication on the 12 iconic buildings
of Norwich, we didn't appreciate what a huge success the Norwich
12 project would be – nor did we anticipate winning two regional
publishing awards for best factual publication and best tourism guide.

Spurred on by this, we felt it was about time the largest collection
of urban medieval churches north of the Alps was properly celebrated.
The wealth and richness of heritage resources in Norwich has almost
hidden this remarkable set of churches, which are compelling not only
in historical and architectural terms, but also because of their profusion
in a relatively compact area. Unless we reveal this heritage 'secret' to as
wide an audience as possible, however, one of our potentially brightest
lights will remain hidden under a bushel.

There have been books on the Norwich churches before, so why is
this one special? Without disrespect to the pre-war volume of Claude
Messent, or the more recent publication by Noel Spencer, we are aiming
at something rather different. First, the text has been written by Nick
Groves, an acknowledged authority on the subject who brings a rich
and scholarly interpretation to the set. Second, we have added a series
of stories that inject anecdotes and experiences into the buildings,
bringing the architecture alive. Third, we have sourced some of the
images from HEART's medieval churches photography competition,
reflecting how the buildings are viewed and valued by local people
today. Finally, we have worked with local agency East Publishing, who
have already helped us secure two awards. They have guided us on
design and production to deliver a high-quality product.

As with the Norwich 12 project, we have worked with partners
to ensure that we make the most of the set. While bodies such as
the Diocese of Norwich, the Norwich Historic Churches Trust, The
Churches Conservation Trust and tenants including Hungate Medieval
Art wrestle with the challenges of making medieval churches work on
a daily basis, we hope that HEART can support them in a coordinating
role, and that this book in particular will help to highlight how very
special the 'set' of Norwich churches is.

We have also developed interpretive sign boards outside a significant
proportion of the churches, produced leaflets on individual churches,
supported the development of a website, produced an exhibition on the
whole set, funded a churches ranger and supported individual churches,
such as St Julian's and St Peter Hungate. We hope that this integrated
approach will not only help to sell one of Europe's sensational sets
of ecclesiastical buildings, but will also raise the profile of one of the
world's great heritage cities in the public consciousness.

About this book

Nicholas Groves

There has been no book dealing specifically with the churches of Norwich since the publication in 1970 of *The Old Churches of Norwich*, by Noel Spencer and Arnold Kent. This was a somewhat idiosyncratic work, giving random snippets of history and notes on the architecture, but in no systematic form. It was illustrated with some very good monochrome pictures, and in many cases these are invaluable records of the appearance of the interiors of the churches just before many of them were closed. It was brought out in a revised edition in 1990, with new pictures, but the text was not always accurately updated (for example, it refers to the rood screen in St John Timberhill, which had been removed in 1980).

This book, while acknowledging its debt to Spencer and Kent, is a new work, and I have attempted to make the information more uniform, describing the exteriors of the buildings, their interiors and principal monuments, and adding some history. In the case of the redundant churches, I have included pictures of their interiors before they were closed.

Much of the text that appears here is based on a series of leaflets I wrote for Norwich HEART and the Norwich Historic Churches Trust (NHCT), which were produced for the city's Heritage Open Days in 2007 and funded by the Paul Bassham Trust. The leaflet text also formed the basis of each church's entry on the NHCT website. In this book, however, I have been able to expand the information, especially in terms of the historical content.

I have also departed from Spencer and Kent in not including the Old Meeting House or the Octagon Chapel, as I have taken as my remit the medieval churches of the city of Norwich. (Having said that, a book dealing with all the chapels and meeting-houses of the city is long overdue.) On the other hand, I have included some notes on the three churches that were lost in the 1942 bombings and not rebuilt – St Benedict, St Michael-at-Thorn and St Paul – as there is plenty of documentary and photographic evidence about them, and St Benedict's tower is still standing. Likewise, I have included St Peter Southgate, demolished in 1887, but whose tower still stands in part; St Bartholomew Ber Street, largely demolished in 1549, though much of it was still standing until the 1950s and a large lump of its tower still stands in Ber Street; and St Crowches, mostly demolished in 1551, but whose chancel was discovered, during demolition work, to be still standing in 1838, serving as a public house. It was demolished, but not before a drawing had been made of it. Finally, I have also included brief notes on the city's other 'lost churches', demolished in the 1540s and earlier. *November 2009*

Introduction

Norwich is frequently described as a 'city of churches', although this title could well be applied to several other towns, of which the city of London is the most obvious. It does have a good number, and once had even more. What is important about them is that they form the largest collection of surviving medieval churches in any European town north of the Alps.

The exact number of churches in pre-Reformation Norwich is debatable: much depends on how they are counted. Certainly there were not, as the popular saying has it, 52: "one for each Sunday" (nor were there 365 pubs, "one for each day" – there were over 500). Some churches were demolished before others were built; one (St Helen) was demolished and the parishioners accommodated in part of the church of the new hospital of St Giles; and archaeology has revealed the remains of at least two that have left no documentary trace at all. So, counting all the churches that are known to have existed, the number is closer to 63. This compares with the 126 of the city of London, and in a smaller area.

Why so many?

There are various theories as to why there should be so many, when two or three churches could probably have catered for the whole city. Ultimately, the reason is lost to us, but it is possible to note that towns which grew up around the same time as Norwich (i.e. in the 11th century) seem to have many small parishes, while towns growing up a century later tend to have one large parish. Besides London, other comparable towns with many churches are Thetford, with 22; Lincoln and York, with 47 each; Oxford with 20; Exeter with 29; and Winchester, which rivalled Norwich with 57. In all cases, they now have far fewer: Thetford, for example, has been reduced to three, of which only one is still in use as a church.

One theory states that there was a decision to build many small churches to serve many small congregations, but examination will reveal usually that the population of the parishes was far smaller than the number the church could hold. One part of the answer may lie in the fact that many of the churches were owned and founded by lay people: we know that in 1086, 12 burgesses held the church of Holy Trinity in Norwich. We know also that St Giles-on-the-Hill was founded by Elwyn, a thane. Churches were treated as pieces of property, and were subject to all the wrangles that other real estate is. St George Tombland, as late as 1272, was given to the College of St Mary-in-the-Fields by John le Brun,

the founder of the college; he must have owned the church. One indication of this is in the 'surnames' of some churches: in London, St Mary Woolnoth = Wulfnoð; St Nicholas Acon = Haakon. These would possibly be the names of the founders or owners of the churches. (This does not happen in Norwich, however; the surnames are all descriptive.)

Another theory that has been put forward for both London and Canterbury takes us back to the question of the dedications. In 1973, Albert Haussling advanced the theory that in post-Carolingian Gaul, the multiplication of altars in monastic churches was not, as is usually stated, to accommodate the growing number of priests who each had to say mass daily, but to provide for the cults of specific saints (although this was why more and more monks became ordained). It was to improve the supernatural patronage; the more saints that were venerated, the better. Thus, as the big Romanesque monasteries grew up all over Europe, they had, in addition to the expected Lady Chapel, other side-altars dedicated in honour of various saints, local and otherwise. This can be clearly seen at Norwich Cathedral Priory, with its various chapels and altars. What Haussling realised was that these dedications included those of the churches of Rome, e.g. John Baptist, Lawrence, Clement. Thus the monastery church becomes a microcosm of the city of Rome, another home for those saints who protected the Eternal City – and thus the Empire.

In Metz, the dedications spread beyond the walls of the cathedral (Peter and Paul, Mary, Michael, John Baptist, Lawrence, Clement). When Augustine came to England in 597, among other things, he brought a collection of relics of Roman saints, which were in due course sealed into the altars of the churches of London and Canterbury. As John Halliburton says, "Somehow, the Tiber had flowed into the Thames". London has (or had) many Roman dedications: Agnes, Augustine of Canterbury, Clement, Dionis, Gregory, Helen, Lawrence, Pancras, Peter, alongside several each to Mary and Michael, as well as some Apostles. There are also local British saints: a good mix of Anglo-Saxon (e.g. Dunstan, Mildred, Edmund), Celtic (Bride, Alban) and others brought in for various reasons (Nicholas, Christopher, Martin).

This pattern is even more marked in Canterbury, where Eric Cambridge has argued that the patron saints were deliberately chosen to "recall arrangements in and around the city of Rome". So the cathedral dedication (Saviour/Christchurch) echoes that of the papal cathedral in the Lateran; the extra-mural monastery (now St Augustine) of Peter and Paul reflects the two great apostolic cults. There was once a church dedicated to the Four Crowned Martyrs, again reflected in Rome and a very rare dedication elsewhere in medieval Europe; likewise St Pancras.

So, does this work for Norwich? Even though there was no cathedral until 1094, it must be remembered that the city is a Saxon construct, and may thus reflect these arrangements. Norwich Cathedral is dedicated to the Trinity, although it was often known as Christchurch, picking up the dedication of a parish church that it replaced. Among the churches, there are several dedications each to Mary, Michael, John Baptist and Peter; there are Lawrence, Gregory, Augustine, Helen and several apostles. There are plenty of local (i.e. English) saints: Edmund, Ethelbert, Etheldreda, Cuthbert; there is a Christopher and several Martins, and so it is possible that the number of churches was driven not by how many were needed to accommodate the people, but by how many saints needed to be commemorated. (Presumably having more than one dedication to the same saint made doubly, or trebly, sure of their aid…)

The churches today

There are now 31 churches standing, of which at the time of writing, only eight are in use as parish churches, 18 under the care of Norwich Historic Churches Trust, three under that of The Churches' Conservation Trust, and one in private ownership. Closures and demolitions have been relatively conservative over the years. In the early Norman period, Trinity (or Christchurch) was lost when the Cathedral was built on its site, and one or possibly two others (dedications unknown) were lost to the Castle, while St Michael Tombland was deliberately closed and demolished. St Ethelbert was severely damaged in the riot of 1272, and replaced by a chapel over the

Ethelbert Gate of the Close. St John the Evangelist, St Matthew-at-Palace and St Margaret Newbridge were lost as a result of depopulation after the Black Death; St John Colegate and St Michael Conesford were incorporated into the precincts of the Black and the Austin Friars, respectively. The major closures took place immediately after the Reformation, in the 1540s, when 14 churches were closed and demolished. No more were lost until 1887, when St Peter Southgate was closed and pulled down. St Simon and St Jude was closed in 1892, and was saved from demolition in the 1920s. Four were lost to bombs in 1942, of which only St Julian was rebuilt.

The Brooke Report of 1971 recommended the redundancy of the majority of the remaining churches, which happened in 1973. Three more have closed since then: St John Maddermarket (1981), St John-de-Sepulchre (1984) and St Augustine (1997).

The vast majority of the surviving churches are built in the Decorated or Perpendicular styles of architecture: or, more commonly, a mixture of both. A few traces of Romanesque styles remain, notably at St Julian and St Etheldreda. There is no major 'Early English' fabric, which is why the Duke of Norfolk specified it as the style for his new Roman Catholic church (now Cathedral) of St John. All the churches were reordered internally at various dates during the 19th century, and thus where furnishings survive, they are likely to be Gothic revival, in line with the dictates of the Ecclesiological Society, and not one interior with box-pews and galleries survives. The two St Georges retain (appropriately) a good deal of their Georgian furniture, but even St George Colegate, which best retains a Georgian feel, has east-facing bench seats, made out of the old box-pews (many have been removed), the inscriptions on the reredos (Decalogue, Creed, Lord's Prayer) have been painted out, and the pulpit has been lowered. The sole non-Ecclesiological interior is at St Helen, and as that functions rather more as the chapel of the Great Hospital than as a parish church, it was less likely to be subject to liturgical fashions.

Late 20th-century work in the 'working' churches is, on the whole, minimal. St John Timberhill had a major reordering in 1980; varying amounts of pew-benches have been removed in a number of churches, especially St Giles and St George Colegate (both aisles), and St George Tombland (north aisle and rear of nave).

As we have seen, the Brooke Report of 1971 recommended the closure of all but five of the churches; in the event, St Peter Mancroft, St Stephen and St Andrew were left to function as independent parishes, as they still do; St John Maddermarket was also left open, with the understanding that it would close on the retirement of its rector, which happened in 1981; it was then united with St Peter Mancroft. All the rest were formed into four united benefices:

Parish of Parmentergate
St Peter Parmentergate was the parish church; St John-de-Sepulchre also remained open until 1984, and St John Timberhill was partially in use until 1980, when it became the parish church and St Peter was closed. St Julian was left, owing to its connection with Dame Julian.

United Benefice of St Giles
St Giles-on-the-Hill became the parish church. It had been united with St Benedict after that church was bombed in 1942, and it further absorbed St Lawrence with St Gregory, and St Margaret-de-Westwick with St Swithin.

United Benefice of St George Tombland
St George became the parish church. It had been united with St Simon and St Jude in 1894, and now also absorbed St Michael-at-Plea with St Peter Hungate, and St Martin-at-Palace.

Norwich Over-the-Water
This parish comprised all the parishes north of the river, and south of the city wall. St George Colegate and St Augustine were left open to serve it. Recent changes have redrawn the boundaries, and St George now serves the area south of the inner ring road and north of the river. North of the ring road, the western portion has been united with St Luke Aylsham Road, and the eastern portion with Christchurch New Catton.

The problem of what to do with the redundant churches was solved by the Diocese leasing them to Norwich City Council, which then set up the Norwich Historic Churches Trust to care for them, and keep them in good repair. The churches under the care of NHCT have all been found new secular uses, and thus their furnishings have, for the most part, been dispersed; only St Clement-at-Fyebridge at present retains its full set of fittings.

Three churches were taken into the care of The Churches Conservation Trust (CCT): St John Maddermarket in 1990 and St Augustine in 2000. Both these retain their fittings intact. St Lawrence was stripped shortly after it was declared redundant in 1968, and now stands as a splendid empty space. After much uncertainty as to its future, it was vested in the CCT in 1992.

The following notes do not pretend to be exhaustive: they cannot be, but it is hoped that they will indicate the main points of interest in the architecture, furnishings (if any) and history of each building. Many of the churches have their own detailed guidebooks, and these will fill in the details.

All Saints

Westlegate, map reference E3

All Saints is one of the five ringing towers in Norwich.
The church underwent a major makeover in the late
Middle Ages and remains the focal point of Westlegate
and All Saints Green

Dedication The feast of All Saints is kept on 1 November, and is intended to allow for the commemoration of all the redeemed, known and unknown, who are now in heaven. Its origin is unclear, but the feast appears to have been observed in England since at least the eighth century.

Exterior The church consists of nave, chancel, north aisle, south porch and unbuttressed square west tower. Documentary evidence for the foundation of the church is lacking, but in the later Middle Ages there was a major makeover of an earlier building. The tower is 15th-century, very plain, without buttresses. Its corners were rebuilt in brick in the 19th century, and the top stage was rebuilt in 1913. The nave windows are in the late 15th-century Perpendicular style; the chancel windows, with pointed arches and curved tracery, are slightly earlier. The large east window is in the 14th-century Decorated style but is, in fact, Victorian.

The porch must have been a later addition because it overlaps the nave plinth. Rougher masonry above its roof shows it was once higher. Rough areas where the west side of the porch meets the nave show there was once a stair turret to the parvise. Beside the last nave buttress on the south wall, the exposed area of flint foundation shows where the rood-stair turret once stood.

Interior During the 15th century, the north wall was replaced by the present arcade of four-centred arches opening into a new north aisle. The south wall was made more elegant by modelling it with arches, and the chancel and tower arches were enlarged. A carved font (now in St Julian's) was placed at the west end of the nave. The bell near the tower screen was cast in 1647 by John Brend II, who had his foundry nearby and is buried here.

From the 1860s until 1973 All Saints was furnished in the high-Anglican tradition. The 18th-century box-pews survived until 1887, when they were converted into open benches; they were replaced by chairs in 1929. There was an elaborate reredos; the Virgin and Child were represented in the window above the high altar (the glass is now in St John Timberhill) and in a statue to the right of the chancel arch. A new rood beam was erected, with a cross on it. Choir stalls were placed in the chancel, and a side altar and an organ in the north aisle.

All these have now been removed, and further alterations made to facilitate its new use. These include a new enclosed gallery in the north aisle, forming a meeting room; a kitchen and servery; and the creation of office space. A gallery (from St Saviour's church) has been placed in the tower to provide a platform for bell ringers (All Saints is one of the five ringing towers of Norwich). Glazed doors have been installed and there is access for people with disabilities. However, the chancel remains a consecrated chapel, and the altar-table is still in place.

Opposite:
detail from
war memorial
window, south
wall of nave

Left: exterior
from the south

Monuments A memorial floor slab of 1735, near the servery, commemorates Elizabeth Cox. A wall monument in the nave to William Clabburn (d. 1812) commemorates one of the leading manufacturers of the famous Norwich shawls.

General The parish, which was in the patronage of the Sculthorpe family, was united with St Julian's from 1706 until 1929; it was then united with its neighbour St John Timberhill. In 1973, the church became part of the new parish of Parmentergate, and was declared redundant. In 1979 it was leased by the Norwich Historic Churches Trust to the All Saints Centre, as a place of Christian hospitality.

Furnishings moved elsewhere The font is in St Julian's. The tester of the Lady altar is in the Lady chapel in St George Tombland. The organ is now at Holy Trinity, Rackheath. The reredos is in East Tuddenham.

Top left: the medieval font pictured in All Saints in 1937 (it is now in St Julian's)

Above: the chancel today, with the altar-table

Right: a 17th-century memorial slab

Below: from All Saints Green, the tower rather dwarfed by the 1960s block

Part of the family

My mother founded the All Saints Centre in the 1970s. She had a real sense of social responsibility and was aware there were a lot of difficulties, such as redundancies, in the city. She had been looking for a venue where she could set up a centre to serve the community, providing Christian hospitality in a street-level kind of way, and was full of ideas. All Saints was made redundant in 1973 and the rest, as they say, is history!

She literally opened the door one day, set up a table and kettle and waited to see what would happen. People donated loads of stuff to help, such as chairs and carpets, and the centre grew with the help of volunteers.

The centre evolves all the time – as the needs of visitors become apparent, the centre tries to meet them. There's a certain sort of hush in a church, a 'getting away from the world' and All Saints works really well for us. The location is super – it really stands as a beacon.

I like to see the centre as a giant sitting room rather than a drop-in centre. All age groups and different types of people come in, perhaps to buy a coffee, sit in a quiet area and read a little or enjoy some live music. My mother liked to say that the centre provides food for the body, mind and spirit. Being a part of it is like being part of a family.

Katherine Gray, Trustee, All Saints Centre

Top left: detail of war memorial window

Left: interior view, 1937

Below: from All Saints Green, 1938

17

St Andrew

St Andrew's Street, map reference D3

Completely rebuilt in 1506, St Andrew's church stands
in the centre of Norwich and contains one
of the finest collections of memorials in the city

Dedication The church is dedicated in
honour of the apostle Andrew, who was
supposed to have been crucified on an
X-shaped cross. It is the only church in the
city with this dedication.

Exterior No trace of any previous church
remains, as the entire fabric was rebuilt in
1506; the name of John Antell has been
connected with it. The church consists of
an integrated nave and chancel, with north
and south aisles, west tower, and north and
south porches. The wealth of the parish can
be seen in the generous use of freestone to
face the building. The new church is bigger
than its predecessor, as it was extended
eastward to the very edge of the churchyard,
and the porches wrap around the tower.
The flushwork frieze around its base was
intended to be visible outside. The porches
may be another addition, as they are built of
flint, and not freestone.

The tower dates from 1478, and now
lacks its parapet, which had pinnacles at
each corner and in the middle of each side.
It was replaced by the very unsightly brick
wall in the 1960s. On the east wall, under
the window, is a row of carved shields. These
are thought to have been transferred from
the previous building. They are possibly
associated with William Appleyard, who
became the first Mayor of Norwich in 1403,
and who lived in the house to the north of
the church, now the Bridewell Museum; the
shields' civic importance may have ensured
their survival. The centre shield shows the
Arms of the Passion, and those to its south
are reversed, so that the lions do not appear
to be turning their backs on it (see page
21). The shield immediately to its north,
which had three chalices with Eucharistic
hosts, has been very heavily defaced, as the
doctrine of transubstantiation was deeply
unacceptable at the time.

Interior The whole church is roofed in
one sweep from east to west with a timber
roof of tie-beam construction. The chancel
and its chapels were originally divided from
the nave by a rood screen, which crossed
the building from north to south, and the
doorways to the stairs can still be seen. In
the south aisle windows there are some
fragments of medieval glass, including
Death leading a bishop away: part of the
Dance of Death, which occupied the
clerestory windows.

Nothing else remains of the medieval
furnishings. All the current furnishings date
from the late 19th-century renovations. The
previous pulpit of 1741 (which had been
given by BJ Ellis, the vicar, and stood in the
centre of the middle alley) was removed in
1860. The sedilia were restored in 1841,
which is very early for this kind of work.
The reredos was installed in 1856, and the

Opposite: interior
view, looking
east towards the
high altar

Left: view from
Bridewell Alley,
1938. Note the
parapet on the
tower, but the
pinnacles have
been removed

Left: 19th-century carved choir stalls and organ screen

Below left: monument to Sir John Suckling (photographed in 1937)

Below right: detail from monument

A place of hospitality

I've been involved with St Andrew's for around 25 years and it's really important to my family – one of my daughters married there and my grandchildren have been christened there.

I've always been interested in history and have been a Blue Badge Guide for the best part of 25 years. What I love about St Andrew's is that it's so full of light and space – that's the beauty of it. My favourite part is Suckling Chapel, which is so well known and one of the reasons people come to visit the church.

St Andrew's is known for its hospitality and welcoming visitors, which is evident during Norfolk Churches Trust's annual sponsored bike ride event, when we provide cakes and drinks for visitors stopping by. It takes place during Heritage Open Days, which is always really popular. In 2005 1,000 people came to see St Andrew's over the HODs weekend – I couldn't believe it. That's the atmosphere of St Andrew's.

Ellen Clarke, keyholder to St Andrew's

low stone screen, the pulpit and the seating followed in 1867. The west gallery was removed in 1863. The font is a Victorian replacement of 1878, but its cover dates from 1637. It was found in pieces in the belfry, and is very similar in design to those at the neighbouring churches of St George Tombland and St Michael-at-Plea.

Monuments The church has one of the finest collections of memorials in Norwich. The former chapel of St Anne, in the north-east corner, is the Suckling chapel, and the monument to Sir John Suckling (d. 1613) on the north wall has very complicated symbolism and inscriptions in five languages. Suckling was treasurer to James I, uncle of the poet Robert Suckling and an ancestor of Horatio Nelson.

General After the Reformation, St Andrew's became a centre of Puritanism, as recorded on two boards at the west end of the nave, over the south door. The advowson is in the hands of the parishioners (this was also the case at St Peter Mancroft and St Benedict). Until quite late in the 19th century, the parish held a preaching competition for applicants for the incumbency, and the winner was duly appointed.

Furnishings moved elsewhere The medieval font is now at Walpole. The original organ, built by GP England in 1794, came from the Assembly House in 1808 and was installed in St Lawrence in 1863. From there it went to St Mary's, South Walsham.

Top left: flint galletting (small flakes of flint set into the mortar) at St Andrew

Top right: exterior from the south, showing the rood stair turret

Below left: monuments in the Suckling Chapel

Below right: carved coats-of-arms on the east wall. From left to right: the city, the King and St Andrew

St Augustine

Gildencroft, map reference B2

St Augustine's church is distinguished by a striking red brick tower, which dates from the 17th century, and a highly unusual inscription on its rood screen

Dedication St Augustine's stands rather remote from the other churches of Norwich, partly because the area around it was, until the 19th century, fields and gardens. It is probably dedicated to St Augustine of Canterbury, who was sent to England by Gregory the Great in 597, although there is a possibility it is Augustine of Hippo, or even both.

Exterior The church consists of nave and chancel, with north and south aisles of equal length, south porch and west tower. The most noticeable thing about the church is its red brick tower. This was built between 1683 and 1687, following the collapse of the original tower. The bottom few feet of the tower show the old flint construction, which was retained as a foundation, and some stonework (the sound holes and the gargoyles at the top) were reused. The battlements date from the 1880s. The tower's unusual appearance led to the parishioners becoming known as 'Red Steeplers'. The statement in the second edition of Pevsner – that the original tower was merely faced with brick – is inaccurate.

The rest of the church is built of flint, dating largely from the 15th century, although much was done in the 1880s, when the architect RM Phipson worked here – notably the windows, buttresses and south porch. The nave appears shorter than it is, on account of its tall clerestory, which is not continued into the chancel.

Interior The church is square in plan, with a nave and a chancel of equal length, and two aisles that run their full length east to west. It has been suggested that the nave, being so short and narrow, preserves the footprint of an original Anglo-Saxon nave, although no fabric remains to support this theory.

The roof was put up in about 1530, and is a tie-beam construction. The font is 15th-century. The front of the gallery in the tower is made from the old 18th-century communion rails. The rest of the furnishings date from Phipson's 1880 restoration. Before Phipson's work, the interior presented a very different appearance. Owing to its square plan, the communion table was at the east end (where it remains) but the pulpit and reading desk were at the west end, with the box-pews arranged in between, so that the occupants could see both. This was an arrangement of great practicality, and was introduced in 1846, although the classical altar-piece was removed at the same time. Phipson's refurnishing was in line with ecclesiological ideas.

The screen was erected in 1920, as a memorial to the dead of the Great War; the names of the 79 fallen are inscribed on its west face.

There is little stained glass: the east window is 1870, and the window in the vestry is 1894.

Monuments There are not many monuments, but of interest is the one to Matthew Brettingham (1699–1769), who built Holkham Hall and worked at Gunton Hall and Langley Hall; and one to Thomas

Opposite: exterior from the south, showing the red brick tower

Below: exterior in 1828, as drawn by Sillett. At this date, the nave and chancel were rendered

ST AUGUSTINE, NORWICH. S.E.

Clabburn (d. 1858), a weaving factory owner. The tablet has shuttles on it, and was erected by 600 of his weavers.

General The parish, which is under the patronage of the Dean and Chapter, was united with various neighbouring ones – St Mary Coslany, St George Colegate – over the years, but was finally united with St Luke, Aylsham Road, and the church declared redundant in 1997. The church came under the care of The Churches' Conservation Trust in 2000.

The list of names on the rood screen starts with John Abigail, who was shot for desertion, aged 20, during the First World War (1914–1918). Although the names of such men are now being added to memorials, Abigail's name was placed on the list when the screen was made and, because of his surname, comes first. This is an extremely rare, if not unique, occurrence.

Clockwise from top left: interior, looking west, showing the memorial screen; the sanctuary and east window (1870); detail of stained glass window; exterior from the south-east, showing the contrast between the brick tower and flint church

National treasures

My interest in English parish churches dates back to when I first came to this country as a student in the mid-1970s, when I was overwhelmed by their beauty and variety. I love this country and working for The Churches Conservation Trust (CCT) is one way of making sure that our national treasures are conserved, studied and passed on for the enjoyment and inspiration of future generations.

On every visit to Norwich, I'm struck by just how much wonderful medieval architecture there is in the city. The CCT owns three churches in Norwich, of which St Augustine's has been one since 2000. The declining congregation simply could not afford the money required to restore the 17th-century brick tower, so they started to use the church hall for services instead. As a result, the church was declared redundant and vested in The Churches Conservation Trust by the Church Commissioners.

To appreciate St Augustine's, you have to understand it in the context of the history of this part of Norwich. I am fascinated by its unique red-brick tower, completed in 1687, which earned its parishioners the nickname of the 'Red Steeplers'. So far the CCT and Norwich City Council have ensured that the church and churchyard are in a good state of repair. We're glad 1,000 visitors visit the church each year and services are still held from time to time.

There's more we can do to develop increased use, with the advice and involvement of local people. Most importantly, we're determined that our churches should once again be the living centres of the communities around them. We want people to love, use and be inspired by all our churches.

Loyd Grossman,
Chair of The Churches Conservation Trust

"On every visit to Norwich, I'm struck by just how much wonderful medieval architecture there is in the city"

Below: exterior from the south-east, taken in 1937

St Clement-at-Fyebridge

Colegate, map reference C3

St Clement's is believed to be one of the first churches in Norwich to be erected on the north side of the river. Records show that it was once an important parish, to which other city churches paid tithes

Dedication The church is dedicated to St Clement, usually said to be the fourth Bishop of Rome, who was martyred at the end of the first century: he was tied to an anchor and thrown into the sea. Clement is thus a patron of seafarers, and was very popular with the Danes; it is known that there was a Danish ('Viking') settlement on this side of the river. The church is surrounded on all four sides by footways, forming an 'island site', a characteristic that tends to mark out important churches of Anglo-Saxon foundation.

Exterior The church consists of nave, chancel and west tower. The present nave replaces an earlier, narrower one, the quoins of which are visible – embedded in the west wall on either side of the tower. The church has no porches, although it is possible that the rougher flintwork round the south door may be the remains of one, now incorporated into the widened nave.

The chancel, nave and tower are all in the Perpendicular style and probably date from the early 15th century. However, the Decorated style of the east window of the chancel, if it is not a Victorian insertion, suggests an earlier date for that part of the building. The nave is wide, without aisles, relatively short, and has a low pitched roof, making it look rather heavy: the former, narrower nave with a steeper roof would have been better proportioned. The tower, on the other hand – with corner buttresses at the four stages and a battlemented parapet decorated with flushwork – is most elegant. The tower clock has a fine classical frame, but is somewhat mismatched with the medieval belfry window that it partly covers.

Interior On both sides of the chancel the wall arches enclose deeply recessed windows or sections of blank wall. Do these represent an attempt to refine earlier thick and irregular walls? Also of this date is the chancel roof, with its arched bracing and its

wall posts supported on corbels carved with angels bearing shields, two with trumpets. The font is in the Perpendicular style, and carved with flowers and leaves.

The furnishings all date from the 1889 restoration by HJ Green, when the west gallery (installed 1846), double-decker pulpit and box-pews were removed. The present furnishings include benches with attractively carved panels on the ends, which form a set with the carvings on the pulpit and the font.

Monuments In the floor of the nave is a brass memorial to Margaret Petwoode, dated 1514. A large floor slab just inside the main door, from which the brass has been removed, is very possibly the remains of the memorial of the wife of Edmund Wood, referred to by Francis Blomefield in his history of Norfolk. Wood became mayor in the mid-16th century and is recorded as having been buried "before the aulter of Our Lady". He almost certainly built and lived in the magnificent house on the corner of Fye Bridge Street and Fishergate, 'rediscovered'

Below: drawing by Sillett in 1828. The spirelet has since been removed

Opposite: view from the south-east, showing the unusual width of the nave; clock face, showing dates of restoration; memorial brass to Margaret Petwoode (d. 1514)

ST CLEMENT.

HOC MONUMENTUM
PATRIS ET MATRIS
MATTHEI PARKER ARCHIEPISC CANTUAR
TEMPORIS INJURIA PENE DELAPSUM
REFICIENDEM CURAVERE
PRISCI BENEFACTORIS HAUD IMMEMORES
MAGISTER ET SOCII
COLL: CORP: CHRISTI CANTAB
A D MDCCCXXIII

in 1990 and now called the King of Hearts. His son Robert, who also became mayor, was buried in the chancel. He welcomed Queen Elizabeth I on her visit to the city, but the festivities went on so long that he had to "forbear the utterance of…his Oration because it was about seven of the clock and Her Majesty had then five miles to ride". He had to content himself with presenting it to her in writing, whereupon she "made him a Knight [and departed] with the Water standing in her eyes".

The walls have many monuments to the Harvey and Ives families. These two families provided many of the city's mayors in the 18th century, and were much intermarried. The Ives were wool merchants and the Harveys merchants and bankers.

In the south churchyard is a box-tomb inscribed to the memory of the parents of Matthew Parker, Archbishop of Canterbury under Queen Elizabeth I, although it is a 19th-century reconstruction. In 1549 he preached here against the "hurliburlies" of Kett's Rebellion. He left money for an annual sermon in the church, which still continues.

General The living was in the gift of Mendham Priory, and eventually passed to Gonville and Caius College after the Reformation. The church stands close to Fye Bridge, the river crossing of the major historic north-south axis of the

city (King Street/Magdalen Street). The church is thought to be one of the first in the city erected on the north side of the river, possibly as early as 1040, although no architectural evidence from this period is visible. One fact that points to the parish's importance is that there was a large detached portion of it outside the walls (which became the parish of Christchurch New Catton in 1841). A number of other churches nearby also paid tithes to St Clement's, suggesting it may have been the original parish (a 'minster' church) from which the others were carved.

In the later 19th century St Clement's became one of the principal Ritualist churches, apparently changing almost overnight from extreme evangelicalism. Following redundancy in the 1960s, the church was used for counselling and pastoral work, which enabled it to retain all its furnishings.

The Reverend Jack Burton first preached here in 1969 and was inspired by the peacefulness. Eight years later he took the unusual step of asking the Norwich Historic Churches Trust whether he could personally rent the church. For more than 30 years Jack opened St Clement's every day for private prayer and meditation. He also held a number of services, the most memorable (and lively) of which was the annual Christmas Midnight Mass.

Above: 19th-century tomb commemorating the parents of Archbishop Matthew Parker, who were buried in the churchyard in the 16th century (photographed in 1938)

Opposite (from top): the south-east corner of the nave; the font; exterior view from the north-east, 1934

An oasis of calm

I've been associated with St Clement's since 1969. At that time the Methodist Church and the Church of England were expected to unite – I was a Methodist Minister working as a bus driver and was permitted to be attached to St Clement's parish. When St Clement's was made redundant in the early 1970s I continued to clean it and generally look after it and eventually I was allowed to hire it from the Norwich Historic Churches Trust. St Clement's gave me a base for my unconventional ministry but above all it was open every day. Today I'm retired but I still hold keys for the Trust and open the church regularly to visitors.

I care deeply about the old churches of Norwich. They are oases of quiet sanity and places of reflection. Churches aren't just townscapes and exteriors. They are interiors and ambience – sacred spaces for deep thought and places which make you think. St Clement's has a very powerful ambience and atmosphere, which I attribute in part to its great antiquity. It's not the largest or the most dramatic of Norwich's medieval churches but, I promise you, it's one of the most potent. There's something to be experienced there – it's a special place where 1,000 years of prayers have seeped into the walls.

I find the light particularly interesting. Daylight breaks from the east and I've been stunned by this in the mornings. In the evening the golden light comes through the tower window and lights the nave, which is very impressive.

The Reverend Jack Burton

St Edmund

Fishergate, map reference B4

Named after the 9th-century king of East Anglia,
St Edmund's church was founded in the late Anglo-
Saxon era and was once a centre for pilgrimage

Dedication The church is dedicated to St Edmund, the king of East Anglia.

Exterior The church consists of nave, chancel, south aisle and chapel, and south porch. There is also a south vestry. It is one of the smaller churches in the city and, as it stands, is entirely Perpendicular, although its dedication would indicate a foundation of late Anglo-Saxon date. The tower has a distinctive outline, and the size of the buttresses and the flat parapet suggest it may have been intended to stand higher. The north porch is very humble, and is merely a structure to cover the doorway. It is somewhat dwarfed by the vestry to its east, with its Victorian Gothic chimney. Between them is the rood-stair turret. The south aisle, which runs the entire length of the nave and chancel, was built in 1463.

Interior The interior has long been completely emptied of its furnishings, which were by Edward Boardman and dated from the restoration of 1882. Until then, the church had retained its 18th-century fittings, of which the semi-circular pediment of the reredos survives, fixed to the vestry wall. The fittings were remarkable in that the communion table was at the east end of the aisle, not the chancel. In the centre of the nave roof is a large carved and coloured boss, which is all that remains of the medieval interior. The boss has been damaged, but shows the arms of St Edmund, with the arms of St George to either side, and those of the Cathedral Priory above; a fourth shield is missing. The boss has a Latin inscription: *S. Edmundus, Flos Martirum, velut Rosa, vel Lilium* ('Saint Edmund, Flower of Martyrs, like a rose or a lily'. The first four words are now lost). A west gallery was inserted in 1990.

Usually, an aisle was built against the wall of the church, which was then pierced by an arcade, allowing the church to remain in use for as long as possible during construction work. Here the piercing is highly idiosyncratic: it is a series of arches with expanses of wall in between, which are themselves pierced by large niches, which possibly held statues.

Monuments The church has only four monuments. One is to the Maltby family: Charles junior (d. 1790) was an eminent surgeon in Norwich who lived and worked in the parish of St George Tombland; he gave the church its clock.

General In the Middle Ages, St Edmund's must have been quite a significant church, as it possessed a portion of the shirt in which the saint was killed, making it a centre of pilgrimage. The offerings probably funded the rebuilding. An attempt was made in the parish in the 1830s to revive the flagging textile industry, but it came to nothing and the area became increasingly run-down. Worship ceased in the 1950s, and the church was used for storage purposes. It became increasingly dilapidated until the NHCT restored it, and today its primary use is as the Norwich Pregnancy Crisis Centre. The Gateway Vineyard Church also uses the building (which it calls the Fishergate Centre) for its Sunday meetings, playgroups and other activities.

St Edmund St Edmund was the king of East Anglia, 855–869. He was killed by the invading Danish army. According to Passio he was shot to death with arrows and then beheaded, although the account in *The Anglo-Saxon Chronicle* implies that he fell as he fought the Vikings on the battlefield. The head was guarded by a wolf, which may be a reference to Edmund's dynasty, the Wuffings. Edmund was the patron saint of England until displaced by St George in the 1340s. His shrine in the abbey at Bury St Edmunds was one of the richest in the country. It was destroyed at the Reformation, as were all shrines.

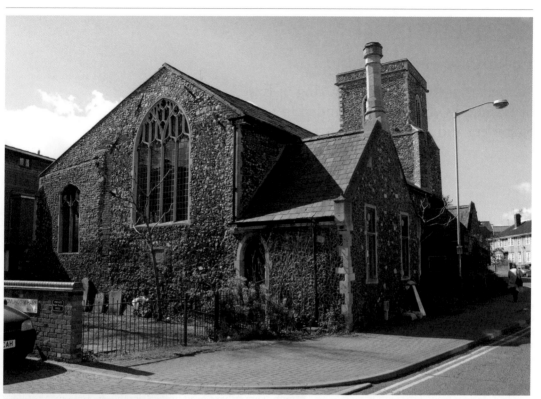

Above: exterior view from the north-east, showing the break in the fabric where the aisle is joined on

Left: interior, looking west, 1938

Below: exterior view from the north, 1950s

The life of St Edmund

The patron saint of England until the 1340s, St Edmund was king of East Anglia from 855 to 869. Only 14 when he ascended to the throne, for much of his reign he was involved in a desperate struggle to protect his kingdom from raids and settlement by Danish Vikings. He was killed, in battle or soon after, by the invading Danish army .

According to his life story, written in the 10th century, he was tortured by being shot with multiple arrows until stuck "like a porcupine". He was then beheaded and his head was thrown away into the undergrowth in disrespect, where it was found by a wolf. Instead of eating it, the wolf held the head between its paws and protected it until Edmund's people could recover it. They were able to locate the wolf because the head called out to them in its own voice, saying "I am here!"

St Edmund was a hugely popular saint in early medieval England, and his shrine at Bury St Edmunds was one of the richest in the county. Pilgrims on their way there could stop at St Edmund's church in Norwich to venerate its relic of St Edmund.

Sophie Cabot

St Etheldreda

King Street, map reference F5

Now a thriving artists' studio, St Etheldreda's
dates back to Norman times. It underwent
a major restoration in 1883 to create an idealised
'medieval' church

Dedication The church is dedicated to
Etheldreda, one of the four daughters of
King Anna of East Anglia, all of whom were
canonised. Etheldreda founded a monastery
on the Isle of Ely, which was the precursor
of Ely Cathedral, and died there in 679.
The Abbots of Ely had to provide men for
the garrison of the castle in Norwich, and
this church may have been attached to the
lodging that was built for them.

Exterior The church consists of nave,
chancel, south porch and round west
tower. The lower, round part of the tower is
original. The octagonal belfry is a rebuild of
1723, though much of its outer facing is by
Boardman. The south porch was added in
the 15th century, in the Perpendicular style.
Above the doorway are the coats of arms
of its donors. The niche was for a statue of
St Etheldreda. The fine, inner round-arched
doorway is the Norman original, though
much restored.

On the outside of the nave and chancel,
the Norman zigzag string course either side
of the inner doorway continues outside and
is a clue to the layout of the original church.
To the left, on the present corner buttress,
it marks the original south-west corner
of the nave. To the right, broken by later
windows, it stops at a flat Norman buttress,
the original south-east corner of the nave. It
then drops to a lower level, marking the start
of the original, probably apsidal, sanctuary.
It finally stops at a modern buttress, which
marks the start of the later, rectangular
chancel that replaced the earlier apse.

On the north side of the nave, there is a
larger window in the Perpendicular style of
the late 15th century. Unlike a similar one
on the south side, it escaped the restorers'
attentions. To its east, the area of rebuilt
flintwork marks the site of the former rood-
stair turret. Further to the west, the Norman
zigzag string course reappears and then
curves to form a window arch, now blocked.

From this it can be assumed that the church
was originally lit by a row of single-light
round-headed windows at this height.
Below it, at a lower level, is a 15th-century
doorway, also now blocked.

The chancel was refaced by Boardman,
and it is easy to see where his work ends and
the original is left: the carefully-faced flints
are of the 19th century. The large Decorated

Below: interior,
looking east,
1937

Opposite: the
round tower,
with the
octagonal belfry
stage of 1723

Above: the chancel door in the north wall

Left: the font in 1938

Below: exterior view from the south, 1964

east window by is also by Boardman, and replaces a plain wooden one, which was probably inserted in the 17th century.

Interior Nothing apart from the thick walls now hints at the original Norman interior. The tall tower arch, replacing a smaller Norman one, was inserted probably in the 13th century. A wide chancel arch would also have been built at this time, but the present one is by Boardman. The present upper floor provides a close-up view of Boardman's fine nave roof. The wall beams on which it rests are probably 15th-century. The chancel roof dates from the early 20th century.

A wall-painting of St Christopher was uncovered in 1884, and a drawing of it was made, but the painting itself did not survive. The doorway, now blocked, on the north side of the nave (near the chancel arch) gave access to the rood-stair turret. Following the 1882 restoration, the church was furnished in what was thought to be a medieval style, under the influence of the Oxford Movement.

Monuments There are only three. In the chancel is a monument to William Johnson, who died in 1611. It was moved from St Peter Southgate church, demolished in 1887. The other two are both early 19th-century, to Robert Smith Riches (d. 1845) and Crisp Brown (d. 1830).

General In 1883 the new vicar, Nathaniel Bolingbroke, initiated a major restoration. The architect responsible was Edward Boardman, and his aim was not the conservative repair of what he found, but the creation of an idealised 'medieval' church. The nave roof was renewed, buttresses were added, flintwork refaced, and windows (where not already of that period) were renewed in the Decorated style of the late 14th century, which at the time was held to be the most 'correct' style. Exceptions are the two south chancel windows, which were copied from what was there before: hence the Y-tracery (which is the clue to the 13th-century date for the chancel). The church had retained its thatch until this date, when it was replaced by tiles. It was the last city church to do so.

The parish was united with that of St Peter Southgate in 1884, and St Peter's was demolished. St Etheldreda's closed when its last vicar, Selby Strong, died in 1961. Residential numbers had been falling, especially after extensive bomb damage in the area in 1942, and by 1970 the church was derelict. It became part of the new parish of Parmentergate in 1973, and was declared redundant. Since 1975 extensive repairs have been carried out. To accommodate artists' studios, an upper floor, north roof light, lavatories and kitchen have been provided.

Furnishings moved elsewhere The organ (18th-century, possibly by Snetzler) and the bell went to St Francis Heartsease in 1962.

A creative space

St Etheldreda Artist Studio was set up in Norwich in 1981 by people from Norwich Art School (now Norwich University College of the Arts). As the first studio group set up in Norwich, it was quite innovative at the time. It is run as a non-profit making cooperative for artists who all have their own space here. We rent the space from the Norwich Historic Churches Trust and share the duties of studio organisation, making and exhibiting artwork.

In the 1980s a mezzanine was put in to provide more space upstairs. There are currently 12 artists and there is quite a diverse skills base. I'm a painter and I've been involved in the Artist Studio for 11 years, but there are also new people who have recently finished degree courses or are currently studying. Most of us also have other jobs.

The studio is now very well established and we have quite a sense of community – we all have our own little space where nothing encroaches and we can do what we want to do, but also get feedback from people on our work. We open for Heritage Open Days, for exhibitions and events like Open Studios. Visitors say what a lovely use it is for the church.

Cora Shearing, Treasurer, St Etheldreda Artist Studio

Below: interior, looking east, showing subdivisions for artists' studios

Right: wall monument to William Johnson (d. 1611), contrasting with contemporary artwork

St George Colegate

Colegate, map reference C3

The magnificent nave clerestory and interiors of
St George's reflect the wealth of its parishioners in
former times, many of whom were rich cloth merchants

Dedication This is one of two medieval churches dedicated to St George in Norwich, which may indicate its foundation date, as dedications to St George tend to be late, usually after the First Crusade of 1096.

Exterior The church consists of nave, chancel, north and south aisles, north and south chapels, north and south porches, and west tower. As it stands, the church was built between 1459 (nave) and 1513 (south aisle and chapel). The north chapel was built by William Norwich, mayor in 1461, and may well be by the mason John Antell, who worked at the Cathedral, and possibly at St Martin-at-Oak. The clerestory was glazed in 1514. It is the nave clerestory which attracts notice: it is tall and of freestone, which bears witness to the wealth of the parish at that time. The south porch has good, but decayed, carvings in its spandrels: one of the Annunciation, and the other of St George being armed by angels. The chancel dates from around 1498.

Interior Inside, this church is the one that most retains its Georgian atmosphere, and again, the furnishings speak of the wealth of the leading parishioners, who were cloth merchants. There is a large west gallery, erected in 1802 for the organ. Built by George Pike England, the organ is one of the very earliest to be installed in a parish church in Norwich. The pulpit is late 18th-century, with a backboard and tester, and an elegant staircase. Although the tester remains at its original height, the pulpit was lowered when the seating was altered. The latter now consists of open benches, which were cut down from the old box-pews in 1899. The benches in the aisles were removed in the 1960s. The reredos is of 17th-century style, but of 18th-century date. Its panels originally contained the Creed, the Lord's Prayer and the Ten Commandments, and the gilt ornamentation is of cast lead. The font is

from St Saviour, brought here when that church closed.

The church is flooded with light from the clear glazing in the late Perpendicular windows. The only coloured glass is in the east window. This is supposed to be a copy of Reynolds' glass at New College, Oxford, but is very badly decayed.

Monuments St George Colegate has one of the largest collections of monuments and family memorials in Norwich, including many examples of work by craftsmen from the Norwich School. In the north chapel is the chest-tomb of Robert Jannys, mayor in 1517 and 1524. It is of terracotta, and by the same craftsman who worked on similar monuments at Oxburgh and Wymondham. At the east end of the south aisle is a memorial to John Crome, the landscape artist. An unusual one is a ledger-slab by the font, which tells of the murder of Bryant Lewis on Thetford Heath in 1698.

General St George's is now the only church north of the river that is still used for worship. It is also one of the five ringing towers.

Opposite: the tower, seen here from the west, closely resembles those of St George Tombland, St Clement and St John-de-Sepulchre

Below: St George's from the north-east, as drawn by Sillett in 1828

ST GEORGE, COLEGATE.

37

John Crome, 1768–1821

Crome, romantic painter and founding figure of the Norwich School of artists, was the son of a weaver. He was born in Norwich in 1768, and baptised at St George Tombland. He is known as 'Old Crome' to distinguish him from his son, John Berney Crome, also an artist.

Crome was apprenticed to a coach or sign painter, although he is supposed to have acquired his skills by copying the Gainsboroughs and Hobbemas owned by Thomas Harvey of Old Catton, his patron. His success was such that he was appointed drawing master to the influential Gurneys of Earlham, near Norwich, whom he accompanied to the Lake District in 1802.

In 1803 Crome founded the Norwich Society of Artists, which also included John Sell Cotman. He was the society's president in 1808 and again 1821, the year of his death. His many pupils included Dawson Turner's family of Great Yarmouth and Richard Noverre Bacon, who remembered him as "my mirth loving, kind and earnest teacher". Crome worked in both watercolours and oils – the oil paintings alone number more than 300, and are displayed at major galleries around the world, including the Tate Gallery and the Royal Academy, as well as in Norwich itself.

Sophie Cabot

Top: exterior from the south, taken from the old Norvic factory on Colegate

Above: terracotta chest tomb of Robert Jannys

Opposite: interior, looking east from organ gallery

St George Tombland

Tombland, map reference C4

Despite heavy restoration in the late 19th century,
St George's retains many of its Georgian furnishings.
It is also notable for its extraordinary stained glass windows,
including work from the studio of William Morris

Dedication This is one of two medieval churches dedicated to St George in Norwich (the other is St George Colegate), which may indicate a foundation date after the First Crusade of 1096. The suffix Tombland is from two Old English words meaning 'empty land or space', referring to the site of the late Saxon market.

Exterior The church consists of nave, chancel, north and south aisles, north chapel, north and south porches, and west tower. It is built of flint rubble, but the nave clerestory stands out as it is of brick – a high-status material when the church was built in the 16th century. The tower stands out because of a large, blue clock face. The front of the south porch dates from the 1880s, and bears no relation to its original appearance. Its interior vault has some fine bosses, possibly carved by the same masons who were working on the Cathedral bosses.

The organic growth of the building is easy to see: originally it was just a nave and chancel, probably of the 13th century, although the chancel windows are extremely late Perpendicular in form. The tower was built between 1430 and 1450, and replaced an earlier one, which may have been round. The north porch was added in 1445, and the north aisle shortly after that. The scar of the demolished rood-stair turret can be seen at the junction of the aisle and the chancel chapel. The south aisle dates from around 1490, and the south porch from 1495.

Interior It is possible that St George's represents an attempt to reproduce the effect of the new fashionable 'hall churches' of the 16th century (such as St Andrew) without going to the expense of a rebuild. The clerestory runs from the chancel into the nave, and the chancel arch has been cut away as far as is practicable. Another oddity is that that nave pillars do not stand opposite each other. This is partly because the west bay of the north aisle is occupied

by the porch, but also because the eastern respond of the north arcade stands very proud from the wall. This was to enable a door to be pierced through the wall above the pillar capital to give access to the rood loft. The pillars and arches are all of brick that has been plastered over, except for the west arch of the south arcade. There was a medieval gallery in the tower (the door is still in place), which held the chapel of Our Lady in the Steeple, one of four of its kind in Norwich. It was removed in the 1880s, along with the 17th-century extension of it.

The church remained 'unrestored' until the 1880s, owing to the long incumbency of Kirby Trimmer (1842–87). The Reverend Walter Crewe (1895–1920) introduced the High Church form of services, which still continues, and initiated a major restoration between 1878 and 1886. In the usual way, the box-pews were replaced by benches, and the west gallery of 1672 was removed, as were two other galleries in the north and south aisles. Despite this heavy restoration, the church retains a good deal of its Georgian furnishings. Principal among these is the reredos, a very fine piece

Below: exterior from the south-east, as drawn by Sillett in 1828

Opposite: the tower of St George's, visible over timber-framed houses in Princes Street

ST GEORGE, TOMBLAND, S.

of the early 18th century. The Decalogue is unfortunately covered by brocade, and the Lord's Prayer and Creed in the side panels were painted over around 1880. The altar, with its gradines and tabernacle, was set up in the 1890s, although the altar-table is of 17th-century date, but much altered. It was further modified in the 1960s to accommodate a medieval *mensa*, or stone altar-slab, which had been discovered in the basement of a house in Elm Hill.

The pulpit is 17th-century, and possibly of French workmanship. It has extremely delicate foliage carving on the front panel. Its tester may be older. Close examination of the staircase reveals how it was cut down from the original 'three-decker'. The aisle benches are made of wood recycled from the old box-pews. (The benches in the north aisle were removed in 2008.)

The font is 13th-century and made of Purbeck marble. Its cover is 17th-century, and very similar to those at neighbouring churches St Michael-at-Plea and St Andrew. Beside the font is a stone bread-table, used for giving out bread to the poor. There is a coloured relief carving of St George, which is probably German, of about 1530, in the north aisle.

There is a good deal of glass, including two medieval roundels in the south-aisle window and two 17th-century Flemish panels set high up in the north aisle. The Magnificat window (east end of south aisle) is by the studio of William Morris. The extraordinary mosaic windows in the north aisle are of the 1860s, and may be the earliest surviving Victorian coloured glass in Norwich.

Monuments The church is extremely rich in monuments. The principal ones are: Mary Gardiner (1748, north wall of sanctuary), by Scheemaker; Thomas Anguish (1617, beside the organ), by Nicholas Stone; John and Olive Symonds (1609, above the bread-table), now lacking its surround.

General In 1633, William Bridge was appointed vicar (for more biographical information, see entry for St Peter Hungate).

Top: exterior from Tombland Alley

Above: detail from the Magnificat window

Left: monuments to John and Olive Symonds (1609) and Francis Stone (1835) at the west end

Above: the statue of Our Lady of Walsingham and mosaic window in the north aisle

Below: interior view, looking east, 1937

Thomas Anguish

In the church is a memorial to Thomas Anguish, who was born in 1536. With his wife, Elizabeth, he had nine sons and three daughters. Anguish became a highly valued and respected member of the congregation and local community, and served as both Sheriff and Mayor in Norwich. He died in 1617 and in his will left property to be used to set up and found a children's hospital. His legacy lives on today in Anguish's Educational Foundation, a charity giving educational grants to young people in Norwich.

The memorial to Anguish, his wife and children is somewhat hidden by the Victorian organ. It is carved in alabaster by Nicholas Stone, master mason to Charles I and James I. People say it is wonderful. It shows the couple and their children kneeling, with seven of the children depicted with skulls, as they predeceased their parents. You can also see a crest of the Guild of Mercers – in his lifetime Anguish went from grocer's boy to the Guild of Mercers, which is not bad! Anguish left £10 in his will for the monument, but its eventual cost was £20.

Peter Callan, verger

St Giles-on-the-Hill

Upper St Giles, map reference D1

St Giles has the tallest church tower in Norwich and, as its name suggests, rises from the city's highest ground. Historically, the parish had strong connections with the medical profession

Dedication The church is dedicated in honour of St Giles, a hermit who died around 710, and who is patron saint of the disabled. This was one of the three large parishes that comprised the French Borough, together with St Stephen and St Peter Mancroft. 'The hill' refers to the church's situation on the highest ground in Norwich, which is 85 feet (26 metres) above sea level.

Exterior The church consists of nave and chancel, north and south aisles, south porch, and west tower. As it stands, it was built around 1400. The church is made of knapped flints, apart from the ashlar-faced two-storey south porch, which was added in the 15th century. It has a frieze of running tendrils and crowned letter Gs (for Giles). There is ashlar decoration on the buttresses. The 113-foot (34 metre) tower is not only the tallest in Norwich, but rises from the

highest ground. A beacon was placed on top of it in 1549, and the iron basket for the fire is still on view inside. It was replaced by the current cupola in 1737, and the beacon was replaced by an electric light in 1970. The tower contains a peal of eight bells, the earliest dating from 1430. The tower has two sets of belfry windows (the lower ones now blocked), suggesting that the top stage of the tower was either an afterthought, or was added when the money became available.

Interior The porch has a fan-vaulted ceiling, unique in Norwich. This is at least 100 years later than the nave, as is the door leading into it. The parvise was originally a chapel to St Christopher.

The sense of height and space in the nave is accentuated by the tall, slender piers, which support high rising arches, above which are the clerestory windows. The chancel arch is surrounded by niches for

Left: exterior view from the east, from the City Hall tower

Opposite: the 15th-century south porch

Above: St Giles' bells, photographed during rehanging in 1932

Right: exterior, looking west, with the famous wisteria in foreground

Memories of a bell ringer

My parents were members of St Giles church and I was a member from 1955 to 1961, when I married and moved away. I was one of several parishioners who used to ring the tolling bell every evening – I think the churchwarden drew up a rota. We would ring the date and then 100 rings at 9pm in summer and 8pm in the winter. We would pull on a rope from the ground level of the church then lock it up with a big key and take the key to the vicarage on Cow Hill.

Julia de Salis

images, of which two have been restored. The carved angels in the hammerbeam roof covering the nave hold the shields of England and France. On the ends of the pews, five mace stands remain, from past mayors of the city who were resident in the parish, with their coats of arms. The clerestory has rather small windows, when compared with the slightly later ones at St Peter Mancroft and St Stephen. The font is only partly original; it was damaged in the 1866 restoration, and only the bowl and part of the pedestal were saved.

There is a lectern of 1493 at the front of the nave, brought here from St Gregory (and before that from St Miles Coslany in 1776). It is one of fewer than 50 surviving examples, and is probably of Norwich, or at least East Anglian, make. Its inscription dates it exactly. Others can be seen at Southwell Minster (recovered from the lake at Newstead Abbey), Newcastle Cathedral and Urbino Cathedral in Italy.

The original chancel was demolished in 1581 on the order of the patrons, the Dean and Chapter, to save the cost of its upkeep. The chancel arch was blocked, and the Perpendicular east window was reset in it. The present chancel, in the Decorated style, dates from 1866, and was paid for by the vicar, William Ripley. It was designed by RM Phipson, and is shorter than the original. It has an arch-braced roof. The east window is art of Phipson's design. The reredos is a memorial to Richard Courtier-Foster (vicar, 1927–1933) and was erected in 1957. It was moved forward from the east wall in 2007, to form a sacristy behind it.

Also in 1866, the rest of the church was reordered: the box-pews were removed,

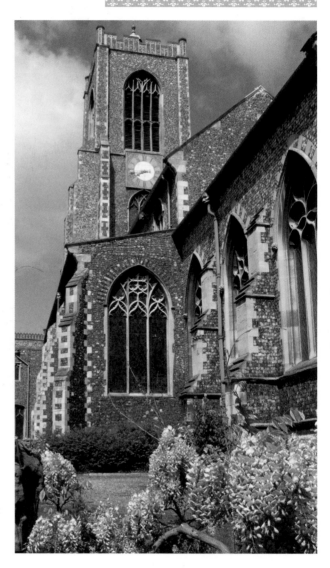

as was the west gallery, and the wall monuments were rearranged.

The benches in the side aisles were removed in 1936, and those in the nave were reset as movable benches in 2008, again contributing to the sense of space.

Monuments Many of the existing houses in St Giles Street were once the homes of prosperous doctors, and the church has a number of wall monuments to them. Of special note is the one to Thomas Churchman (d. 1781), by Thomas Rawlins, at the east end of the south aisle, and the rococo memorial to William Offley (d. 1767), maker unknown, at the east end of the north aisle. There are brasses on the nave floor to Robert Baxter (1424) and Richard Purdaunce (1436).

General The church was reputedly founded by Elwyn the priest, on his estate, and the original church may have been his hall. As noted above, the parish was noted for its medical connections, and in 1886 six of the eight medical staff of the Norfolk and Norwich Hospital lived in St Giles, together with another eight physicians and surgeons.

The curfew John Colton, who died in 1497, was making his way back to the city one night when he lost his way. He was saved from being drowned by hearing the bells of St Giles, and by following their sound was guided to safety. In thanksgiving, he bequeathed to the parish a piece of land, known as Colton's Acre, on Earlham Road, next to the Mitre pub. In accordance with his will, the curfew bell is rung every night.

Above: medieval eagle lectern

Below left: the children's corner in St Giles today

Right: the memorial brass to Robert Baxter and his wife (1424), as drawn by Cotman in 1814

St Gregory

Pottergate, map reference D2

St Gregory's nave and chancel together form one of the best medieval interior spaces in Norwich. The church was the focus of conflict between rival doctrines in the 19th century

Dedication The church is dedicated in honour of Gregory the Great, Bishop of Rome from 590 until his death in 604. He is credited with codifying the melodies used in church services, which is why they are known as 'Gregorian chant'. He was also responsible for sending Augustine to evangelise the Anglo-Saxons.

Exterior The church consists of integral nave and chancel, with north and south aisles, west, north and south porches, and west tower. The church occupies the whole of its site from east to west, and the open space to its south was once part of its churchyard. The exterior presents a uniform appearance, as the church was totally rebuilt (apart from the tower) in the 14th century. It consists of a chancel and nave without structural division, with north and south aisles running the full length except for the easternmost bay of the chancel. There is a west tower, flanked by north and south porches. There is a west door with small porch, and a passageway under the east end of the chancel; the altar space is consequently raised on seven steps. The short tower was surmounted by a spire until 1840; the foundation timbers remain in the belfry. The whole construction is of flint with freestone dressings.

Interior The porches are each of two bays, with ribbed vaults; the south porch has bosses showing St Gregory teaching a music class.

The nave and chancel were rebuilt in 1394, and together form one of the best medieval interior spaces in Norwich. The Cathedral Priory was the patron of St Gregory's, and paid for the rebuilding of the chancel. The aisle windows, though retaining the pointed arch of the Decorated style, have Perpendicular-style tracery. They are known to be by Robert Wodehirst, who also worked on the Cathedral, and pair up with the windows in the north walk of the

Cathedral cloister, which was finished in 1430. This is a rare instance of being able to identify the mason who worked on a parish church. The roof is original. It is simple and almost barn-like, but with carved bosses and angel corbels. They were once coloured, like those in the south aisle.

The bowl of the late 14th-century font is supported by angels who look down on the heads of grotesque creatures at the base of the stem: their bodies are being crushed by it, representing the annihilation of sin in baptism. The elaborate carved wooden cover is 17th-century.

The tower vault has carved corbels, from which the vault springs. There is a bell hole in the centre of the vault. The tower arch and the high vault of the ringing gallery are an even more splendid version of the lower vault that supports the gallery. The tower is probably the oldest part of the building. The blocked round openings in the belfry, not visible on the re-faced exterior, are thought to be Saxon.

The 15th-century wall paintings in St Gregory's have been recognised as being some of the very best in England. The St George and the Dragon painting in the north aisle was discovered by chance during the 1861 restoration. The Four Doctors of the Church in the south aisle were discovered in 1979, but were not fully uncovered and conserved until 1999. The surviving fragments include most of St Gregory, the face and other fragments of St Ambrose and the spindle-back chair of the stall of St Jerome. Nothing of St Augustine of Hippo survives. During the conservation of the Four Doctors, a painting of the Annunciation was also found in the same area: the Virgin Mary, the face of God and the Spirit coming down like a dove, as well as fragments of Gabriel's wing, can be clearly seen.

In the sanctuary is a row of misericords,

Opposite:
St Gregory
from the south,
photographed
from the City
Hall tower

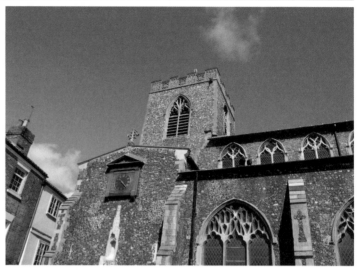

carved with a lion, a bearded man sitting on his haunches and two angels. The altar-table is the memorial to the men of the parish who died in the Great War.

In the south aisle there is a 17th-century fretwork royal coat of arms and fragments of at least three layers of post-Reformation text painted on the wall.

The church was reordered in 1861, when the gallery, classical reredos and box-pews were removed (the first Norwich church in which this happened), choir stalls were put in the chancel and the organ (acquired 1856) moved there from the west end.

Most of the stained glass is from the late 19th century, and is by J and J King of Norwich. The best of the Victorian windows is at the east end of the north aisle, almost hidden by the organ. Fragments of 15th-century glass can be seen in a panel in one of the north windows.

Monuments A number of monuments in the church have been designed by sculptors renowned nationally, as well as those who built their reputation in the Norwich School. These include Sir Peter Seaman (d. 1715), by Thomas Green of Camberwell, Joseph Chamberlin (d. 1762), attributed to the Ivory workshop, and Mary Bateman (d. 1721), by Robert Singleton.

Of particular note is the two-part monument to Francis Bacon (d. 1657), sculptor unknown, now in the south chancel chapel: it consists of a tomb-chest and a wall monument above. Bacon was Steward of Norwich in 1639 and Recorder in 1642. In the same year he was appointed a judge to the king's bench and knighted. The monument is not in its original position: it is known that many monuments were moved around during the 1861 reordering.

General St Gregory is quite certainly

one of the minster churches of Norwich, as the neighbouring parishes along St Benedict's Street all paid tithes to it during the Middle Ages. In the 17th century it was noted as a church where Laudian ideals of ceremonious worship were followed, and in the 19th century was a centre of conflict when the vicar, William Sharpe (1851–64), introduced Ritualist worship: he emptied the church as a result. This trend was reversed under the next vicar, but then picked up again, and St Gregory went on to become one of the leading Ritualist churches in the city.

The church became redundant in 1973, and the parish became part of the united benefice of St Giles. A 14th-century door-closing ring (often mistakenly called a sanctuary knocker) and a 16th-century bell were placed in the care of the Castle Museum. A 15th-century eagle lectern (bought from St Miles Coslany in 1776) was moved to St Giles' church, where it is still used. Post-redundancy alterations include

Above left: a 'jigsaw' of medieval glass, reset in the north aisle

Above right: the tower and south porch from St Gregory's Green

Below: the interior today from the tower gallery

the insertion of lavatories in the north porch. Since redundancy, the church has been in almost continuous use as a centre to promote the arts.

Furnishings moved elsewhere The lectern is in St Giles-on-the-Hill, as is the statue of St Gregory. The hanging rood is at Easton. The 1856 organ was moved to St Margaret-de-Westwick in 1887, and then to Little Barningham in 1975, where it remains.

Purity and personality

St Gregory's Centre for Arts has been around for three years as a centre for the community, for music, art and education. Within this historic building we aim to provide a friendly atmosphere for members of the community; to help people to find access to the arts, related employment and education; to provide a mentoring and advisory service; and to make art and crafts available to all without discrimination or exclusion.

The acoustics are exceptional, as the relationship between the height of the original 14th-century roof and the length of the church helps to give purity and resonance to sound and music here. There's also a wealth of 17th-century wall monuments and statuary, and the 500-year-old wall paintings are of national importance. But it's the sheer personality of St Gregory's as a whole that is its greatest value.

Rosamunde Woods, Curator,
St Gregory's Centre for Arts

Above: detail from the George and the dragon wall painting

Below: the east end, from the Strangers' Hall garden

St Helen

Bishopgate (The Great Hospital), map reference C5

St Helen's is at the medieval heart of the Great Hospital complex. The panelled ceiling of the 14th-century chancel, now the Eagle Ward, is ornately decorated with 252 spread eagles

Dedication The church is dedicated in honour of Helen, the mother of the emperor Constantine. She is credited with discovering the remains of the cross on which Christ was crucified. The story that she was born in these islands is unfounded. However, the hospital itself is dedicated to St Giles.

Exterior The whole church consists of chancel, nave, with north and south aisles, south transept and a western tower, but the parish church itself comprises only the eastern part of the nave and aisles, and the south transept. As it stands, the church was rebuilt in various phases. The tower was under construction in 1375; the chancel was rebuilt by Henry Dispenser in 1383, and the rest in the later 15th century.

Interior The only part that is easily accessible is the area serving as St Helen's church, which consists of three bays. The furnishings are virtually untouched by the late 19th-century reorderings that happened elsewhere. The seating consists of benches in the nave, of which the ends at least are medieval. The one on the south side at the east end has a fine carving of St Margaret emerging unscathed from the belly of a dragon. It commemorates John Hecker, Master of the Hospital, 1519–32. In the aisles, facing inwards, and also across the east end, are box-pews with a two-decker pulpit as the focal point. The preservation of this very old-fashioned arrangement may be due to the long incumbency of William Patteson as vicar, from 1824 to 1881.

The transept still functions as a 'communion chapel', and contains the altar, which is a Stuart table. Behind it is a classical-style reredos, with the Creed, the Lord's Prayer and the Ten Commandments. The transept has a lierne vault of 1480, with 24 bosses showing scenes from the life of the Virgin. It is very close in style to those being erected in the Cathedral at the same time. The transept also has a pew built by Thomas

Ivory (1709–79) "to be convenient for his family and servants", dated 1780.

General The original church of St Helen stood across the road. In 1249, Bishop Walter de Suffield founded St Giles' Hospital "in remission of my sins", to care for "decrepit" priests and for seven poor scholars. St Helen's church was given to the hospital in 1270 and was demolished; the eastern part of the nave of the hospital church became, and remains, the parish church, while the western four bays formed the infirmary hall. The chancel was effectively the chapel of the hospital, and was divided from the rest by a rood screen. At the Reformation the chancel and the infirmary hall were walled off from the church. The chancel was partitioned horizontally, and both floors became accommodation for the female residents. It has a panelled ceiling, decorated with 252 spread eagles, which may have been painted in honour of Anne of Bohemia, who visited Norwich in 1383 with her husband, King Richard II. The infirmary hall was also partitioned, and became the men's wards. The hospital was dissolved at the Reformation, and was acquired by the City Corporation. It was refounded as the Great Hospital, to care for older Norwich residents with limited means.

Below: exterior from the north-east, as drawn by Sillett in 1828

Opposite: the church tower from Bishopgate

ST HELENS, CHURCH and HOSPITAL.

A social history of Norwich

On the days when the buildings are open to the public, residents at the Great Hospital are often asked to man St Helen's church, the cloisters and the Eagle Ward, alongside the trustees. When you live here, you become so involved and want to share that with others.

Visitors are always interested in the way people lived happily in Eagle Ward – you can't compare it with the accommodation facilities we have today! They are also interested in the age and the layout of the church, and the graves – which give you a social history and understanding of relationships, early death and so on. Visitors also love the quietness and the way people have worshipped here for so many years.

We have an annual service in May to commemorate the Great Hospital and say prayers in thanks to Bishop Suffield who founded it. In recent years a resident wrote a new hymn for the service, previously there wasn't anything appropriate. We now sing it every year, to the tune of *Amazing Grace*, as a new tradition.

It's wonderful to have the church so close for residents. It must be incredibly rare to have a medieval church on the site of a residential care home. St Helen's itself is so extraordinary and even people at the Great Hospital who don't come to church are inordinately proud of it.

Great Hospital resident

Top: interior of the 15th-century Lady Chapel, showing 17th-century communion table, 18th-century reredos and 19th-century communion rails

Above: window showing St Helen, the patron saint of archaeologists

Left: St Helen's from the south

Opposite: the cloister of the Great Hospital; bench end featuring St Margaret emerging from the belly of a dragon – a memorial to John Hecher (d. 1532); St Helen's interior today, looking east towards the blocked chancel arch

St James Pockthorpe

Whitefriars, map reference B4

St James's was a popular meeting place for societies of every kind in the late 19th century. Today the church is the home of Norwich Puppet Theatre

Dedication The church is dedicated in honour of James the Greater, one of the 12 apostles. Pockthorpe has long been a suburb of Norwich, clustered round the Bargate, just to the east of the church. Although it formed a separate parish, dedicated to James the Less, another of the apostles, it had no church, and the inhabitants had to attend this one.

Exterior The church consists of nave, chancel, south aisle and chapel, south porch and west tower. The tower is the memorable feature of this church, consisting of a brick octagon (of 1743) sitting on a flint cube, all resting on the west end of the nave. The whole of the church as we see it now is of Perpendicular date, and consists of a nave, a chancel and a south aisle that runs the whole length of both, but with no clerestory.

The south porch opens into the nave, suggesting that it pre-dates the aisle. Its parapet was rebuilt (to a different design) in the 20th century. It had been given a Classical makeover, and had three figures perched upon it, one of which still remains as a pinnacle on the south-west corner. The rebuild restored a Gothic appearance. The windows are all Perpendicular, except for the east window, which is Decorated.

Interior The structure of the tower is immediately apparent on entering. It sits on three arches (east, south and north) at the west end of the nave, forming a kind of narthex. As these line up with the north and south doors (and the later south porch), it would have allowed processions to pass through the building. The aisle has four-centred arches, with octagonal piers. The chancel roof is arch-braced, while that in the nave is scissor-beamed. Restorations took place in 1842 and again in 1882, when fashionable 'medieval-style' furnishings were inserted, including a screen and Gothic reredos.

Furnishings moved elsewhere The furnishings have all been dispersed. The font, probably 14th-century, is now in the daughter church of St Mary Magdalen, Silver Road. It is octagonal, with two saints on each face of the bowl and a further eight around the stem. A similar one, from All Saints' church, is now in St Julian's. Also in St Mary's is the dado of the medieval rood screen, with 10 fine paintings.

General The parish of St James was a notorious slum area in 19th-century Norwich, dominated by the Pockthorpe brewery. It was one of the earlier churches to adopt High Church ritual. The parish magazines reveal that, in the late 19th century, societies of every kind met there every night of the week. It was the first parish in which sisters from the Community of All Hallows at Ditchingham came to work (mainly on the pastoral side).

The church was closed in 1972, and in 1982 was converted for use as a puppet theatre. An octagonal extension was built on the south side to provide storage and working space.

Opposite: St James from the south-west, showing the unusual tower; puppets displayed against a window of St James

Below: exterior from the south-west in 1938, showing figures on the porch parapet, which are now lost

Above: carved support at the north-west corner of the nave

Left: the medieval font, now at St Mary Magdalen on Silver Road

Below: the interior, looking east (photographed in the 1930s)

Norwich Puppet Theatre

In 1978, when the Puppet Theatre took over the church, it was just a shell, as it had stood redundant since 1969. Looking for a base for the Theatre, Ray DaSilva, our founder, looked at three churches: he chose St James for its location and visibility. Archaeology carried out during the conversion work revealed some of the building's secrets, including the rood staircase and original threshold stone, now visible through a glass panel.

The building has been adapted for the theatre. Nine inches of soundproofing was added to eliminate noise from outside, and the theatre seats come from an old cinema in Cardiff. They're covered in excess or unwanted bus-seating fabric, sewn by upholstery students at Norwich City College. Very hard-wearing!

Today we are one of only two puppet theatres in England (the Little Angel in Islington, London, is the other one) and we show glove, rod and shadow puppet shows. The building is listed and the theatre is not purpose-built, so some visiting puppeteers can get a little frustrated with its quirkiness, but it's good that churches are being used. In many ways they lend themselves well to performing arts. The building is a beauty in itself, giving character to the space, and we provide a supportive and friendly place which creates a good atmosphere. People come expecting one thing but find the church has been transformed and that's part of the experience.

We sometimes get visitors who used to worship here and some who are doing family tree research and want to see where their ancestors' weddings and christenings took place. St James' last choirmaster recently came back, as did a couple who married here and were celebrating their ruby wedding anniversary. It really is a unique and special place.

Ian Woods, manager of Norwich Puppet Theatre

Left: the unusual
flint cube tower,
with octagonal
brick belfry
added in 1743

Above: the
south aisle

Below: the
interior of the
nave today,
looking west

St John Maddermarket

Maddermarket, map reference D3

St John's dates back to Anglo-Saxon times. The church is associated with the actor William Kemp, a friend of William Shakespeare, who in 1599 danced from London to Norwich in nine days

Dedication As with all the surviving churches of St John in Norwich, this one is dedicated in honour of John the Baptist. It may be one of the churches mentioned in the *Domesday Book*, where it is called Holy Trinity. 'Maddermarket' is usually understood to refer to the sale of madder flowers for making red dye, although no evidence has ever been found to show that there was such a market.

Exterior The church consists of nave (almost certainly with integral chancel), north and south aisles, north and south porches, and west tower. It has a rather truncated appearance, as there is no structural chancel, making it almost square in plan. The story that the chancel was taken down to allow Elizabeth I access to visit the Duke's Palace (which stood on the site of the multistorey car park to the north of the church) is almost certainly untrue. Like many other churches, it had been rebuilt in the 15th century without a chancel, and the elegant clerestory, being unusually tall, creates the truncated effect. It is faced with freestone, although the rest of the church is of flint.

The porches are incorporated into the aisles. The north porch has very thick walls, and may well be all that remains of the church which stood on this site in Anglo-Saxon times. Its doorway is much more ornate than that of the south porch, possibly because it was the main entrance from the Duke's Palace. It also has a fine rib vault.

The tower, which was altered in 1822, has a processional way through its lowest storey; there is a rib vault with 12 carved bosses. The east window can be dated to the 1320s, and must have been reset from the previous church.

Interior The square plan is immediately apparent on entering. The west bay of the building, between the porches, has been made into a narthex by the gallery overhead, which was erected in 1912 and is a very good copy of the Jacobean style. The choir sang from here.

The dominating feature is the baldachin (canopy) over the high altar. This is almost certainly the one made in 1741 for St Miles Coslany, and removed from there in 1883. It was brought here in 1917, and obscures the Gothic reredos of 1863.

Little of the medieval furnishings survive, but the interior was certainly divided up by screens as we see today, and there would have been a rood screen across the entire church. The aisle roofs contain much medieval work, and that over the Lady Chapel (south aisle) is painted. The north chapel was similar, but has been removed. The nave roof is also basically medieval, although it was heavily restored in 1876, after a gas explosion in the church. Its construction is similar to that of St Peter Mancroft, where coving hides the hammerbeams.

The church was reordered in 1863, and then throughout the 19th and 20th centuries. It was one of the earlier churches to adopt Ritualism in its services, and the surviving furnishings reflect this: many of them were brought here by William Busby, rector from 1898 until 1923. The lectern is 18th-century, possibly Italian, and revolves. The pulpit is of 1863, but its sounding board may be 17th-century. The font dates from the 1860s.

There is a good collection of stained glass. The centre window of the north aisle has some 15th-century fragments, but the rest dates from the 19th and 20th centuries. The north chapel has an Annunciation (1913), by Powell, in the Pre-Raphaelite style; the south chapel has a Tree of Jesse (1916), probably by King of Norwich. The east window is of 1870, and shows the healing of the Centurion's daughter.

Monuments The church has a large collection of brasses, some of which have

Opposite: exterior from the south, showing the top of the tower, which was remodelled in 1822

been mounted on the walls at the west end. There is also a good collection of wall monuments from the 16th to the 20th centuries.

General The church closed for Anglican worship on 31 December 1981, and was used between 1982 and 1990 by the Greek Orthodox Church. It came into the care of The Churches' Conservation Trust in 1990.

William Kemp, the famous comic actor, had an argument with his friend William Shakespeare in 1599, and in an attempt to upstage him, Kemp wagered that he would morris dance from London to Norwich in nine days. He did this and, on reaching Norwich, jumped the wall of St John's churchyard. A plaque now commemorates the site and Kemp wrote about his journey in his book, *A Nine Daies Wonder*.

Left: interior, looking north-east, 1948

Bottom left: detail from the Annunciation window in the north chapel (1913)

A church to cherish

The Churches Conservation Trust (CCT) is the national charity conserving England's most beautiful and historic churches. For our 40th anniversary year in 2009 we held a weekend of 'Birthday Song', with 40 choirs performing in 40 of the most significant historic churches cared for by the CCT. In St John Maddermarket the Norfolk Gallery Quire, which revives the music that was used in Norfolk village churches in the 18th and 19th centuries, held a workshop and concert. They featured hymns, folk songs and readings of pre-Victorian Norfolk villagers, performed in Georgian costume and lit by candles.

My role is to keep an eye on the fabric of the churches, report issues to the conservation manager, liaise with the local community and help to organise events. The focus of the work is principally to maintain the historic buildings and make them available for use by the local community, relying on fundraising and donations.

St John Maddermarket is ideally situated in a busy pedestrian area and already attracts many visitors from around the world. Our aim in the future is to continue to develop the church, increase its opening hours to the public and offer visitors a guided tour of the church.

Owen Thompson, development officer,
The Churches Conservation Trust

Above: exterior from the north in 1938, showing the wall over which Kemp leapt

Right: the clerestory, faced with ashlar

Below left: detail of the painted ceiling of the Lady Chapel

Below right: the north porch

St John Timberhill

Timberhill, map reference E3

St John's interior was dramatically reordered in the late 19th century to 'recreate' how the church might have looked in the Middle Ages. The vicar at the time, Edward Ram, also introduced various ritual practices that proved controversial

Dedication Like the city's other churches of St John, this church is dedicated in honour of John the Baptist. It was originally sited just outside the Castle bailey. Timberhill itself was the open area to the south of the church, where a timber market was held.

Exterior The church consists of nave, chancel, north and south aisles, and chapels that run the full length of both, giving it a square plan. Its tower fell in 1784 and was replaced by a wooden bell-frame; this was in turn replaced by the current stone turret in 1877. On the east wall, where the south aisle joins the chancel, there is some long-and-short work, which may indicate a date of pre-1066, although Anglo-Saxon building styles continued to be used for some time after that. The dormer windows are needed to allow extra light into the interior, as there is no clerestory. They also date from the 1870s.

Interior The inside of this church has seen several major reorderings. The medieval arrangements were replaced by those of the 17th and 18th centuries, when the nave and chancel were filled with box-pews, and the aisles with inward-facing seats in raked rows, focusing on the pulpit. In 1871, Edward Ram became vicar, and he set in train a thorough reordering inside and out. At this time the church was in a very poor condition, so much so that services had to be held under the gallery for fear of falling roof timbers.

Ram attempted to recreate what he thought the interior of the church would have looked like in the Middle Ages. The square pews and gallery were removed, and the bell-turret replaced. The font was moved from beside the altar to the west end, but its cover was not constructed until 1929. Ram also erected a chancel screen, with loft, in 1890, together with a cross on the beam above. In 1893 he added the figure of

Christ to the cross, and the figures of Mary and John. These, together with various ritual practices, such as burning incense and reserving the sacrament for the sick, caused major differences between Ram and the bishop, John Sheepshanks, for the next 12 years.

St John's interior arrangement lasted until 1980, when the church was again reordered. Ram's screen and loft were removed, as were the choir stalls, and the altar brought forward. The current arrangement is as much a product of the 1980s as Ram's was of the 1880s.

The figures on the rood beam were made in Oberammergau. Over the altar is a candelabrum, probably German, of circa 1500; it was given to the church in 1723. The reredos is also from Oberammergau and was installed in 1911. It was shorn of its canopies in 1980, but some parts have been replaced. The pulpit dates from the 1870s. Ram had started to make it himself, but found it too time-consuming.

The amount of stained glass is minimal.

Opposite: exterior from the south, showing the bell turret added in 1877

Below: exterior from the south-west. The tower fell in 1784 and was replaced by the wooden bellframe shown in this drawing by Sillett in 1828

ST JOHN, TIMBERHILL.

Above: interior, looking east, 1937

Right: the controversial rood figures, installed in 1893

Below left: statue of St John (1914)

Below right: detail from the organ screen in the north aisle

The two notable pieces are the panel of Mary in the south nave aisle, by Martin Travers, and originally in All Saints' church next door. It is an early work, dating from Travers' schooldays. Travers also designed the east window in the south chapel, which shows the Ascension, and is from a much later period of his life.

Monuments There are very few wall monuments. The most noteworthy is that for Robert Page (1778) on the north wall of the sanctuary, which he designed himself.

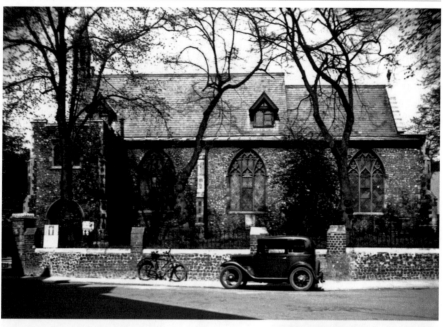

Keeping traditions alive

St John Timberhill stood empty for a few years in the 1970s as it was deemed superfluous. However, when architects said the church tower of St Peter Parmentergate was dangerous, it was decided to close it and move the congregation to St John's. One Sunday the service started in St Peter Parmentergate and then everyone walked in procession to St John Timberhill, where the service was finished! The congregation reordered St John's and turned it into a more modern interior.

Today St John Timberhill is the biggest parish in Norwich and we are open every day, receiving many visitors who really value it. The visitors' book shows people feel it is an oasis of peace.

We are a Church of England church in the Anglo-Catholic tradition – one that stills enjoys the traditional forms of worship and the things that accompany it, like candles, bells, incense, beautiful vestments and so on. The congregation is happy and eclectic – people from all walks of life come from all over the place, as they like the way things are done here. Everyone mixes together. It's remarkable really and everyone mucks in, which is lovely.

Father Martin Smith

Above: exterior from the south, 1938

Right: detail from the Ascension window, by Martin Travers, in the south chapel

Below: interior, looking towards the north-west corner

St John-de-Sepulchre

Finkelgate, map reference G4

During the Reformation, St John-de-Sepulchre's stained glass was replaced with clear glass and its wall paintings were whitewashed. But in the late 19th century, the interior underwent a 'medieval' makeover

Dedication The church is known to have existed before 1066. It was originally dedicated to St John the Baptist, but probably around the time of the First Crusade (1096) it gained an extra dedication, to the Holy Sepulchre. Strictly speaking, it is now called the Church of St John Baptist and the Holy Sepulchre, but everyday use has cut this down to St John-de-Sepulchre, or even just St Sepulchre.

Exterior The church consists of nave, chancel, north and south transepts, south porch and west tower. The well-proportioned, 27-metre high tower has a crisp silhouette with each stage stepping back from the one below. The elegant flushwork parapet and pinnacles date from 1901. The clock face is 18th-century, and the weathercock commemorates the Peace of Utrecht in 1713.

The two-storey north porch has two friezes of shields over the doorway. The alternating letter 'I' stands for Iohannes (John). Above is an elaborate niche for a statue. The porch flintwork is knapped and squared, and the corner pinnacles start below the roof line. The stair turret to the parvise blocks the window jamb, as if it were an afterthought. The uniform nave windows, in the 15th-century Perpendicular style, have a strong vertical emphasis in the tracery. The flintwork of the west wall of the north transept is very rough, and there is evidence of a blocked opening, suggesting that it is part of an earlier structure. (Taylor and Taylor suggest that both transepts might be Anglo-Saxon, but this is unlikely, if only because there is documentary evidence that money was left to build the north transept, in the style of the south one, in 1536.) The door is 19th-century. The corner of the chancel has been chopped back to allow for heavy market-day traffic. The chancel windows have flatter arches than those in the nave, which indicates they are of a later date.

A massive brick arch at the end of the nave, above the chancel roof, was built to reduce the weight on the chancel arch inside.

Interior The porch has a vaulted ceiling, and the carved inner door is medieval. In the nave, mock arches frame the windows and connect the walls visually to the fine timber-framed roof overhead. The entrances to the tower and the two transepts are marked by tall, narrow arches. The narrow recess south of the tower arch was for storing the staves on which processional banners were carried. The font is an East Anglian 'lion' font, and the maker has had fun carving the lions: they are exceptionally smug! The tall, wide chancel arch appears to have been designed to relate to a higher chancel roof, and its sides were cut back to accommodate the medieval screen. The chancel has a steeply pitched roof. It contains several interesting wall monuments and a medieval consecration cross on the south wall.

The Reformation brought great changes. Churchwardens' accounts from the 1540s indicate how the church was decorated and furnished before and after the changes. Stained glass windows, including one of St Thomas Beckett, were replaced by clear

Opposite: exterior from the north-east

Below: north side of the exterior, 1938

69

The font

The font in St John-de-Sepulchre has a deep, octagonal bowl with angels holding shields and crouching lions carved in relief on alternate panels.

The lion is a common medieval symbol of the resurrection of Christ. The *Liber Bestiarum* or Bestiary, of which the best known example is perhaps MS Bodley 764 in the Bodleian Library of c.1250, tells us that "when the lioness brings forth her cubs, they come into the world dead. She watches over them for three days until the lion, their father, comes and blows in their faces and awakens them to life. In the same way the Almighty Father awoke our Lord Jesus Christ from the dead on the third day." The lions which dominate the decoration of the font are thus potent symbols of baptismal regeneration, as those who pass through its waters are incorporated into the death and resurrection of Christ.

Fonts with similar design features can be found at churches in Bradwell, Tharston, Fritton and Morningthorpe and many other villages throughout Norfolk. It would seem that the St John-de-Sepulchre font is a typical example of what one might call the 'mass-produced' Norfolk font of the second half of the 15th century. These may have been produced to order in a Norwich workshop and assembled on site or carved in situ by a mason working from a pattern book. The workings of this trade have yet to be investigated in a scholarly manner, but the large number of identical or very similar fonts throughout the county indicates some form of late medieval production line.

The Reverend Canon Jeremy Haselock

Top: the medieval lion font, 1937

Above: the north porch, 1938

Right: the reredos of 1914 by Oldrid Scott

glass. The richly coloured screen, with its pictures of saints, was sold along with communion vessels and other plate, and the wall paintings were whitewashed over.

St John's took on a new lease of life under John Joseph Gurney, vicar 1876–90, who was influenced by the High-Church Oxford Movement. The church was reordered in line with what was thought to be a medieval interior, with a painted rood screen, choir stalls in the chancel, an organ and a stained glass window over the altar. Thomas Lord's account of a service he attended in 1884 says that incense was used: if so, it makes St John's one of the earliest to revive its use. The elaborate reredos, by John Oldrid Scott, was erected in 1914.

The church became redundant in 1984, and between 1986 and 2009 was used by an Eastern Orthodox congregation.

Above: exterior of the south side of the nave and south transept

Right: interior view, looking east, 1937

St Julian

Julian's Alley, map reference F4

Nestled close to the banks of the River Wensum,
St Julian is a beautiful and historic church.
Even though it has been rebuilt and is tucked away,
it remains one of the city's most famous churches

Dedication This small church has an international reputation, as it was here that Dame Julian of Norwich lived in the later 14th century. The actual dedication is somewhat vexed. It was generally thought to have been Julian the Hospitaller, who was quite certainly mythical, but if the church is an Anglo-Saxon foundation, it may well be St Juliana, a martyr of the fourth century. When the church was rebuilt after being bombed, it was rededicated in honour of the fourth-century saint Julian of Le Mans, the first bishop of Le Mans, of whom little, if anything, is known.

The building as it now stands dates almost entirely from 1958, when it was rebuilt after suffering a direct hit from a bomb in 1942. There is good reason to believe that a church has stood here since Anglo-Saxon times, although whether the destroyed building was of Saxon date, or Saxon workmanship but post-1066, is difficult to decide.

Exterior The church consists of nave and chancel with north porch. There is a vestry on the site of the south porch, and a modern south chapel (or 'cell'). The north wall of the nave is original, and repairs after the bombing revealed a number of circular windows (oculi), quite high up, which was a standard method of lighting Anglo-Saxon churches. One has been reopened, and another was turned into a round-headed window. Similar windows were found in the south wall of the chancel, although these were not reopened.

The tower, one of five round towers in Norwich, took the hit, and collapsed across the body of the church. It was partly rebuilt, and further heightened by about four feet in 1992, to provide a housing for the bell.

Interior Almost everything in the church dates from the rebuild of 1958. Three things pre-date it. First, the font, which is *c.* 1420, and which stood originally in All Saints'

church; it was brought here when that church closed in 1977. It has carvings of the twelve apostles round the bowl, and eight other saints round the stem. The reredos, placed here in 1931, survived the bomb; it was made in Oberammergau. Finally, the door to the cell, which is a Norman archway. It was in fact the main door to St Michael-at-Thorn, which was also destroyed on the same night in 1942, and never rebuilt. The organ loft was built in 1981. The organ on it, of 1860, is by Henry Jones and came here from Abbess Roding in Essex. All monuments except a couple of floor-slabs were destroyed

Some photographs showing the interior before damage are at the back of the church.

There are two coloured windows, one between the cell and the chancel, showing the Lily Crucifix and Julian; the other, in the opposite wall, shows the seven sacraments. Both are by the firm of King of Norwich.

The cell This was built on what was thought to be site of Julian's cell, although there is no evidence to support this. It was in fact more likely to have been on the north side, and may have been detached from the church altogether. (The flint foundations are

Below: exterior from the north-west in 1961, shortly after rebuilding

Opposite: the interior of the reconstructed cell

This page (clockwise from top left): interior, looking east, 1937; exterior from the east, 1937, showing the tower before bombing; Romanesque doorway brought from St Michael-at-Thorn; detail of the font, brought from All Saints; interior today, looking west

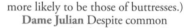

more likely to be those of buttresses.)

Dame Julian Despite common perceptions, the church is not dedicated to her, nor did she necessarily take her name from the church, as Julian (a form of Gillian) was a common name for women in the Middle Ages. Falling ill in 1373, she had a series of visions ('shewings') dealing with aspects of Christ's passion. When she recovered, she became an anchoress at this church, and her musings on her shewings were eventually written down. *The Revelations of Divine Love* is the first known book to be written in English by a woman.

Further information about Julian and her book can be found in the Julian Centre next door to the church.

Above: the partly rebuilt tower, the top few feet and bell cote were added in 1992

Below: detail from the statue of St Mary in the cell

Dame Julian

Julian was undoubtedly the most important of English 14th-century mystics. From the Reformation onward, however, both the woman and her writings were largely forgotten, until the 20th century, when *The Revelations of Divine Love* was retranslated from Middle English. In 1973 the 600th anniversary of the 'shewings' led to considerable international interest. Today she is the most read English mystic – her writing is studied across the world and has been translated into many languages.

Julian lived through the reign of five kings and extraordinary turmoil and social unrest, including war, the Peasants' Revolt and the Black Death. The similarity of her day and the 20th and 21st centuries is striking – I see the social unrest of today and the terrible disparity between rich and poor so like the 14th century. Julian's still assurance in the midst of this is very exciting.

Canon Michael McLean,
formerly rector at St Julian's

St Lawrence

St Benedict's Street, map reference D2

Dramatically sited on a steep incline down to the river, St Lawrence's was a centre of controversy in the mid-19th century. Its Ritualistic services attracted huge crowds, mainly for the spectacle, and there were riots in the streets outside

Dedication St Lawrence (or Laurence) was a deacon in the church at Rome in the third century, but very few, if any, of the details of his life are reliable. He appears to have been martyred around 258, during the persecution of the emperor Valerian, but the tale that he was roasted to death on a gridiron (which became his symbol) is certainly false.

Exterior The church has a very dramatic site. Owing to the steep slope down to the river, on its south side it stands several feet below street level, but on the north an equal height above it: this was made more dramatic in the 19th century when the wall was set back several feet in order to widen the street.

The church consists of nave, chancel, north and south aisles and chapels, north and south porches, and west tower. The most notable feature of the exterior is the unique profile of the tower, with its corner turret. The tower itself is 112 feet (34 metres) high. The nave and chancel, with their clerestory, run without a break under one roof. The clerestory is faced with freestone. There is a very prominent rood-stair turret on the south side, which marks the division between nave and chancel (see below). The west door has two carved spandrels: one of St Lawrence being roasted on a gridiron, and the other of the martyrdom of St Edmund: the abbey at Bury St Edmund's was the original patron of the church. The south door is the original medieval one.

Interior The church has long since been stripped of its furnishings, and now stands as an impressive empty space, flooded with light from the great windows and the clerestory. With the exception of the font, which is 15th-century, all the fittings were of late 19th or early 20th-century date. These fittings include the flight of seven steps up to the altar, and the reredos, which is a war memorial of 1921. It includes painted panels by Kingston Rudd, although

inspection will reveal that many of them are unfinished, and so have a rather impressionistic effect. The figure painting is very much of the period.

The nave and chancel are in fact divided internally, which may indicate that the continuous clerestory is a later addition, to give the effect of a 'hall church', fashionable in the 15th century. The roof dates from 1498. The nave pillars are octagonal, with rounded angles, and their capitals are wavy. There is some medieval stained glass in a mosaic in the east window of the south aisle. The north porch has a particularly fine vault. There were several brasses, but these have been removed to storage.

General From 1811 to 1827, Edward Glover was curate here. His daughter, Sarah, invented the Norwich sol-fa method of singing, which was later modified by John Curwen to form tonic sol-fa (doh, ray, me…). She died in 1867, at Great Malvern, where she is buried. On the east wall of the north aisle there is a brass plaque of 1891 to her memory.

After 1876, the church went into decline and was united with St Gregory in 1903; it

Opposite: the tower from the south-east with its distinctive spirelet

Below: exterior from the south-east in the late 19th century. The steep slope of the churchyard can be seen in the alley to the east

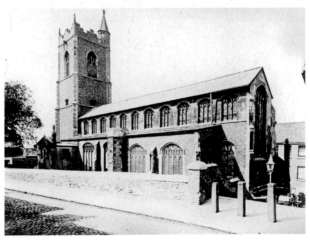

In memory of Sarah Glover

I moved to Norwich in 1964 to take up a position in the music department at the Keswick Hall College of Education, where I taught students about the tonic sol-fa technique for singing, pioneered by Sarah Glover. When I first saw the brass plaque at St Lawrence's commemorating her I thought it looked pretty dingy. I was given a key to the church and have been polishing it every two or three months ever since. I have to stand on a rather rickety chair to reach the plaque, so these days I tend to wait until my son is visiting, so he can stand by and hand me the cloth and Brasso. Then I just get on with it.

Brian Sargent

Clockwise from top left: interior, looking east, 1937; interior, looking east, today; postcard from c. 1864; mosaic window, salvaged from medieval glass in the north chapel

INTERIOR ST LAWRENCE CHURCH, NORWICH.

was finally closed in 1968. After many years of uncertainty about its future (including the possibility of its being unroofed and allowed to become a 'controlled ruin'), it came under the care of The Churches Conservation Trust in 1992.

Furnishings moved elsewhere The organ, brought here from St Andrew in 1863, was enlarged several times. It was restored to its original form in 1971, when it went to St Mary's, South Walsham, where it remains. The statue of St Lawrence is now in St Giles. The church also had several medieval brasses, but they have been removed for safekeeping.

Father Ignatius The church was a centre of controversy in 1863, when the rector, Edwin Hillyard, allowed 'Father Ignatius' (Joseph Leycester Lyne) and his 'monks', who had a house on Elm Hill, to take part in the services. The services were conducted in an extremely Ritualistic manner, with candles, incense and vestments, all virtually unknown in the Church of England at this time. Large crowds attended – mainly for the spectacle – and there were riots in the street outside. One newspaper account of 1864 says that the services were attended by "men of the lowest character", "women with unfeminine faces" and "the occasional respectable person". The church was a solid mass of people, and there was so much laughing and jostling that the reporter was "unsure whether I was in a church or in the gallery of a theatre".

Ignatius left Norwich in 1865, but Hillyard stayed until 1876. By then, the Classical-style reredos had been removed, as had the box-pews (chopped up one night by Ignatius and his cohorts), and the altar steps and the screens inserted.

Above: south side of nave, showing the rood-stair turret. The extensive use of ashlar is a sign of the wealth of the parish

Below: spandrel above the west door showing the martyrdom of St Lawrence

St Margaret-de-Westwick

St Benedict's Street, map reference C2

St Margaret's is now used as an exhibition space, revealing its beautiful proportions. It contains some interesting 18th-century features, including three excellent wall monuments

Dedication The church is dedicated in honour of St Margaret of Antioch, a mythical virgin martyr, who is supposed to have lived in the very early years of Christianity. Among other wonders, she is said to have been swallowed by the Devil, who was in the form of a dragon, but she burst it asunder by making the sign of the cross. She thus became the patron of childbirth, and her cult was very popular. There were 58 medieval dedications to her in Norfolk, of which three were in Norwich: this one, St Margaret Newbridge (on the site of the Playhouse) and St Margaret Combust (on Magdalen Street), both demolished in the 1540s. The suffix 'de Westwick' denotes that this church of St Margaret is in the ward of Westwick.

Exterior The church consists of nave, chancel, south aisle and chapel, north and south porches, and west tower. The tower has a distinctive profile, as the buttresses stop short at the base of the belfry stage, which has windows in the Decorated style. Its north-east buttress is crushed by the nave, which suggests that the nave is later: possibly it was widened. The south porch is crammed on to the west end of the south aisle, suggesting that it was there before the aisle was built. In its spandrels are carvings of St Margaret and another figure among branches. It has an ogee niche for a statue.

The south nave aisle has a string course which continues on to its east face – but not on to the chancel aisle, indicating that they are of different builds – as does the lower roof-line of the chancel aisle. Under the east window of the chancel is a blocked arch turned in brick (about 6 feet x 3 feet/1.8 metres x 0.9 metres), which has the appearance of a blocked doorway. This is a very unusual site for a door, unless it gave direct access to a private pew. On the north side is a plainer porch than that on the south, and a Victorian vestry – its walls

contain the remains of an early carving of the Crucifixion.

Interior The south porch has a tierceron star-vault. The piecemeal development of the church is very evident, as the arches opening off in various directions show. The original church consisted of nave and chancel, to which a south aisle was added, probably in the 15th century. This has an arcade of two arches, with pillars of plastered brick; they have concave sides and rounded angles, as do those next door at St Lawrence. The chancel aisle has pillars of the same style. The nave roof is boarded over, and the chancel roof is plastered. At the east end of the nave is a small doorway, which gives access to the chancel chapel. The stained glass in the east window is by Michael King, and was installed in 1967.

In the tower is a gallery; the front is made out of the old communion rails, and is dated 1707. Also dating from the 18th century is the former reredos (now over the south door), with the Ten Commandments and pictures of Moses and Aaron, conserved in 2008. All other furnishings, including the font, have been removed.

Monuments There are monuments to Anne Rede, who died in 1577, a low tomb chest in the chancel aisle, and three excellent

Below: exterior from the north, drawn by Sillett in 1828

Opposite: interior today, looking east, showing the Ascension window of 1967 and a geometric sculpture by Jeremy Crisp

ST MARGARET. N.

Above: interior, looking east, 1937

Left: the font, photographed here in 1937, is now lost

Right: exterior from St Benedict's Street

18th-century wall monuments to members of the Brown family.

General The fittings were all replaced in 1886 in what was then thought to be the medieval style, and the church was heavily influenced by the Oxford Movement. Services here followed the simpler 'English' ceremonial. The church was closed in 1975, and the furnishings dispersed to other churches. It is currently used as an exhibition space, which enable the proportions to be appreciated.

Furnishings moved elsewhere The organ, which came here from St Gregory in 1882, is now in Little Barningham church.

Opposite: interior, showing the successful gallery conversion; exterior of the south aisle and porch

St Martin-at-Oak

Oak Street, map reference B2

St Martin's was a flourishing church in the late 19th century, and a noted centre of evangelical religion. In recent years it has served as a night shelter for the homeless and is now used as artists' studios

Dedication The church is dedicated in honour of St Martin, the fourth-century Bishop of Tours, who is supposed to have cut his cloak in half to share with a beggar. The suffix refers to an oak tree that once stood in the churchyard and which, in the Middle Ages, housed an image of the Virgin Mary.

Exterior The church consists of nave, chancel, south aisles and chapel, south porch, and the lower stages of a west tower, converted into a west porch in 1953, after bomb damage in 1942. Some of the carved stonework from the battlemented top was reused lower down. There is a west door under a window with Y-tracery, and now a stepped gable. The stair turrets are also very eye-catching – one for the tower itself, and the other for the south porch. The nave has four Perpendicular windows on the north side, while the south aisle has similar ones. This aisle can be securely dated to 1491. It is possible that the mason was John Antell, who was working at the Cathedral. There is no clerestory, and one sweep of roof covers nave and aisle.

The chancel was complete by 1441. It was heavily rebuilt in 1852, though preserving the features of the original, including the Decorated windows and the wall-arches round them on the inside. St Martin's was a flourishing church in the later 19th century, and plans were made for adding a north aisle, but this did not happen.

Interior Unlike many of the other city churches, St Martin's was not part of the Anglo-Catholic movement, but was a noted centre of evangelical religion. Apart from the replacement of the box-pews with open benches, its furnishings remained much the same in 1926 as they had been in 1826.

Nothing of the original furnishings remains. After war damage, the church was refitted for use as a parish hall in 1953, which included adding the extra entrance to the chancel by the rood-stair turret. The chancel arch was bricked in and the chancel retained as a place of worship; the south aisle was divided into a number of rooms. Between the aisle and nave the arcade has four bays, with Perpendicular shafts. The nave roof is arch-braced.

From 1978 until 2004, the church was used as a night shelter for the homeless, leading to further alterations. It is currently used as artists' studios.

Monument The most elaborate monument was to Jeremiah Revans (d. 1727), but this is currently in store.

Furnishings moved elsewhere The organ went to Corton in 1953.

Opposite: the exterior, showing the adaptation of the tower

Below: exterior from the south-west, c. 1910, showing the tower before bomb damage

Opposite (clockwise from top left): the font, 1938; interior, looking east, 1938; a 17th-century carved chair, photographed in 1938, formerly in the church; monument (now in storage) to Jeremiah Revans, who died in 1727

Right: the south aisle arcade, with modern glazing

Below right: interior, looking west

Bottom: detail of monument

A beautiful space for artists

I set up Onoak Studios with Martin Field about five years ago. We had been to Norwich Art School and wanted to carry on practising fine art. We needed studio space and there wasn't much around, so we went to the council and were given a list of empty buildings to look into. We ended up at St Martin at Oak and set up a charity with the aim of supplying studio space. One of our main objectives is to keep Norwich vibrant with art – as soon as people leave the art school [now the Norwich University College of the Arts] they tend to head to London, but we can provide them with space which might encourage them to stay in Norwich. We now have 12 artists using the studios, including potters, painters, sculptors and model-makers.

It's a nice building, but quite problematic. It's too cold in winter, but in summer it's really wonderful and has a nice atmosphere to it. It's a beautiful space and as there's no stained glass, there is complete natural light, which is ideal for painters. It is romantic and feels like an art studio.

Fred Higginson, Director of Onoak Studios

St Martin-at-Palace

Palace Plain, map reference B4

Although many of its 'medieval' features were added in
the Victorian period, St Martin's is without doubt one
of the oldest churches in Norwich, and was mentioned
in the *Domesday Book* of 1086

Dedication The church is dedicated in honour of St Martin, the fourth-century Bishop of Tours, who, as legend has it, cut his cloak in half to share with a beggar. The suffix refers to the fact that it stands just outside the gate of the Bishop's Palace.

Exterior The church consists of nave, chancel, north and south aisles and chapels, south porch and west tower. In general the building as it stands dates from the 15th century, although it is much overlaid by Victorian work. Documentary evidence shows that money was left in 1490 for "the new aisle off the south side of the choir". Most of the windows are in the Perpendicular style.

In 1783 a large part of the tower fell and the upper two stages were not rebuilt until 1874, when the lower part was refaced. The quoins of the tower have an unusual appearance: they are long and narrow, and their white stone contrasts strongly with the dark flint work. In 1851 the north chancel aisle and most of chancel itself collapsed. They were rebuilt in 1853–4, when a thorough 'restoration' of the whole building was undertaken. As a result it is sometimes hard to tell what is medieval and what is Victorian. The two-storey south porch appears to be a 19th-century rebuild.

At the east end of the church the quoins of the chancel are long-and-short work – the long sides of the stones lie alternately vertical and horizontal. This technique is normally associated with Anglo-Saxon work, and is quite certainly an original feature, making this wall one of the oldest surviving pieces of church architecture in Norwich.

Interior The church was converted for use by the Probation Service as a day centre and the interior of the church has been greatly modified to accommodate this in the late 1980s. The nave and chancel remain open, but within is a structure of three decks at different levels, connected by stairs.

The highest deck is level with the first floor of the tower, which contains a kitchen. Underneath the decks, the original floor has in part been lowered to form a sitting area. The nave and aisles are partially separated by cabinets which combine heating and storage. A mezzanine floor has been inserted in the north nave aisle, and both chancel aisles and the lower stages of the tower have been screened off. The conversion has changed the character of the building. But old and new are clearly distinct from one another: the old can still be appreciated while the new has an architectural integrity of its own.

Many of the windows hold good Victorian stained glass by the William Morris workshop and by Heaton, Butler and Bayne. Unfortunately their ornate decorative backgrounds have been removed, leaving the figures 'floating' in large areas of clear glass. A panel of fragments of medieval glass has been set in one of the north aisle windows.

There is a tiny fragment of wall painting beside the east window; there may be more

Below: exterior from the south-west in 1934

Opposite: the tower and south porch, showing the rebuildings of 1783 and 1874

concealed behind the later plaster. In the north aisle there is a panel of black-letter text with strap work ornament, dating from the 17th-century, discovered when a wall memorial was removed. Only two texts remain from what must have been an ambitious scheme of Victorian wall decoration, one over the east window and one over the south door. The latter reads "How dreadful is this place. This is none other but the House of God and this is the Gate of Heaven".

Monuments There are some fine monuments in the church. Of particular note is the chest tomb of Elizabeth Calthorpe (d. 1578) in the north chancel aisle. In the south chancel aisle is a good 18th-century wall memorial above the small doorway. There are also many fine slate memorial slabs in the floor dating from the 17th and 18th centuries, and several older paving slabs that once held brasses, including one very large one at the west end of the nave.

General The church of St Martin-at-Palace is one of the oldest in Norwich.

It stands close to a stretch of the riverbank where traces of some of the earliest settlement have been found, and which was the site of a pre-Conquest market.

The church is referred to in the *Domesday Book* (1086) and excavations made during the conversion of the church in the 1980s revealed foundations of an Anglo-Scandinavian or Norman church as well as evidence of one, if not two, earlier Anglo-Saxon timber churches. The Norman Bishop's Palace and the remains of a Norman house (beneath the Law Courts) are testimony to the high status of this part of the city at that time.

St Martin-at-Palace is now let to the Norfolk Association for the Care and Resettlement of Offenders (Norfolk ACRO), so access is extremely limited.

Furnishings moved elsewhere The organ went to Horsham St Faith in 1974, where it has been much enlarged. A chandelier is now at St Mary Magdalen, Silver Road.

Clockwise from top left: interior, looking east, 1938; the chest tomb of Elizabeth Calthorpe in the north chancel aisle; Victorian wall text over the south door

Fascinating finds

In 1987 there were plans to convert St Martin's to accommodate the Probation Service, and ahead of this we excavated part of the church. The aim was to get an understanding of how it had changed over the years, and of the economic situation and social implications for the city.

We uncovered evidence of an Anglo-Scandinavian or early Norman stone church and of two older timber buildings, probably also churches. The east wall of the stone church survives and is the earliest standing wall in Norwich (dating to about 1060). Other finds included post-medieval burials with remarkable coffin fittings, an early 17th-century wall painting of a biblical text and some early 11th-century fragments of stone from Lindsey in Lincolnshire. The stone had been brought at least 100 miles to Norwich, which would have cost around three times the cost of the stone, so someone at the time had a lot of money.

The Norman House and other remains underneath the nearby Magistrates' Courts had already been excavated and thoroughly documented in 1981, so St Martin's is probably one of the best studied parishes in Norwich, with findings of interest much further afield.

Brian Ayers, City Archaeologist in 1987

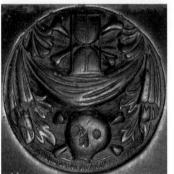

Above: detail from 19th-century stained glass, reset in a clear surround

Left: detail from a ledger slab, with emblems of mortality (skull, crossbones and hour-glass)

Below: exterior, from south

St Mary Coslany

St Mary's Plain, map reference B2

Luke Hansard, the first publisher of the House of
Commons Journal, was born in St Mary's parish and
baptised in the church, which features a 'fashionable'
round tower

Dedication The church is dedicated in
honour of the Virgin Mary, and was once
one of four with this dedication in the city.
The suffix refers to its location in the ward
of Coslany.

Exterior The church consists of nave,
chancel, north and south transepts, south
porch, and west tower. The round tower is
the most striking feature of the exterior.
Round towers were a fashion statement
and have nothing to do with the local lack
of freestone for quoins: it is actually more
difficult to build a round tower than
a square one. They occur in large numbers
in Norfolk and Suffolk, and in a few
other places in England, but they are also
found across the North Sea. Their date
is problematic. This one has triangular-
headed windows, which would indicate
Anglo-Saxon work, but the shafts are of
Caen stone, which would suggest a later
date. These windows had been blocked, and
were only rediscovered when the tower was
reduced in height in 1906: there had been
a Gothic belfry added in the 15th century.
It may well be the oldest of the five round
towers in Norwich. (The others are at
St Julian, St Etheldreda, St Benedict and
the bombed tower of St Paul.)

The rest of the exterior was entirely
rebuilt in the 1460s. The south porch is
1466, with freestone facing and a tierceron
vault inside. It has the usual arrangement of
a niche for a statue between two windows.
The windows are all Perpendicular, with
the exception of a blocked Decorated
one on the north side of the chancel, and
the traces of the original Decorated east
window, not quite obliterated by the new
Perpendicular one. The roof is the main feature.
It is basically the original roof, although it
was much repaired in the 1906 restoration
and again in 1942 after war damage. It is
arch-braced, and the nave and transepts

are treated as one space. They meet over
the crossing with diagonal ribs, centring
on a gilded boss of the Assumption of
the Virgin. There are angels around it.
(Compare a similar arrangement at
St Peter Hungate.)

The medieval interior had a rood screen
across the chancel arch, and probably
screens across the transepts, too. These
were swept away, along with the altars that
stood in the chapels, in the 16th century.
The images that once stood in the niches
halfway along the nave walls, about 6 feet
(2 metres) above the ground, were also
removed at this time.

Monuments The monuments include
one to Peter de Lingcole on the north wall
of the nave. This is dated 1298, and is in
Norman French, recording his bequest to
the altar of the Holy Trinity nearby. In the
chancel are the kneeling figures of Martin
van Kurnbeck and his wife, of 1579.

General The church was restored
in 1857, but by 1890 it was closed and
neglected. It was restored in 1905. After
final closure and redundancy in 1974, the

Below: exterior
from the south,
showing the
medieval belfry
on top of the
tower, drawn by
Sillett in 1828

Opposite: view
from the west,
showing the
round tower and
the triangular-
headed windows
rediscovered
in 1906

ST MARY, S.

92

Luke Hansard

Luke Hansard (5 July 1752–29 October 1828) was an English printer who was born and baptised in St Mary's parish, Norwich. He gave his name to Hansard, the Journals of the House of Commons, which he printed from 1774 until his death. Hansard was educated in Norwich and at the Free Grammar School in the village of Kirton, Lincolnshire. On leaving school at 14, he was apprenticed to Stephen White, a Norwich printer. When Luke's apprenticeship came to an end, he set off for London, finding work with John Hughs in Lincoln's Inn Fields. At the age of 42 Hansard became the sole proprietor of the firm, 26 years after leaving Norwich with only a guinea in his pocket.

Hansard's promptitude and accuracy when printing parliamentary papers was highly valued by the government. His name has been applied not only to the Official Record of the Westminster House of Commons and House of Lords, but to the parliamentary records of many Commonwealth countries, including Canada and New Zealand. There is a memorial to Luke Hansard at St Giles-in-the-Fields Church, London, and his name lives on in the work of the Hansard Society, established in 1944, which began by reporting the most important elements from parliament in an accessible way, using the records of Hansard as the source of its information. Today the society continues to be non-partisan and promotes the ideals of the parliamentary system of government as a research and education charity.

Kate Egglestone, Hansard Society

church went through a variety of uses, including an arts and crafts centre, and an antique market. It is currently used by a publishing firm.

The other furnishings, though still referred to in the revised Pevsner volume, have been removed and dispersed. Parts of the organ are now in the instrument at St Augustine.

Top: interior, looking east, 1937

Above left: exterior from south side, 1937

Right: detail of the chancel roof

Opposite: exterior from the north-east; interior today, looking west

St Mary-the-Less
'The French Church', Queen Street, map reference D4

Almost completely hidden from view, St Mary's has
a fascinating history. It is associated with several different
religious congregations, including the Norwich 'Strangers',
French-speaking Walloons and Swedenborgians

Dedication The church is dedicated
in honour of the Virgin Mary and was
once one of four in the city. The suffix
'the Less' differentiates it from the other
three: St Mary Coslany, St Mary Unbrent
(demolished in 1546) and St Mary-in-the-
Marsh (closed and partially demolished in
1564). Exactly what 'the Less' refers to is
unclear: it may well be in distinction to the
College of St Mary-in-the-Field (on the site
of the Assembly House), which was known
as St Mary-the-Great.

Exterior The church consists of nave,
chancel, south porch and west tower. It is
surrounded on three sides by more modern
buildings, which stand on its churchyard.
This makes it easy to miss the small
entrance (the south porch) tucked away
between the various estate agents and other
offices on Queen Street. Most of the north
side is visible by going into the housing
development through the arch on the west
side of Tombland.

The tower is very distinctive, as the
belfry windows are blocked with red brick,
which contrasts with the black flint of the
rest of the tower. It has no parapet, and
probably never had one. The basic outline
of the tower suggests that, had it been
finished, it may have been similar to towers
such as those at St George Tombland and
St Clement-at-Fyebridge, which are of 15th-
century date. There are two windows of
Decorated date in the chancel, although the
east window is Perpendicular. The nave also
has two windows, but with 19th-century
Y-tracery. The chancel roof is 15th-century.

Interior All the medieval furnishings
have long been removed. It is not known
how it was furnished for the Walloon
church, nor for the Swedenborgians. The
Catholic Apostolic furnishings are recorded
in George Plunkett's pictures, and it is
not clear where they have gone; the lamp-
stands either side of the altar are now

in St George Tombland, where they stand
by the lectern.

General Saint Mary's was one of
the churches closed in the wake of the
Reformation, but unlike most of the others
it was not demolished. The parish, which
also includes that of St Cuthbert, was
united with St George Tombland.

In 1565 the city authorities arranged
for 30 households of religious refugees
from the Netherlands to settle in Norwich.
Called 'Strangers', they were weavers
who knew how to make specialist cloth,
which became the trade Norwich excelled
in. The church of St Mary-the-Less was
given to them as a cloth hall. Some of
the later Strangers were French-speaking
Walloons and they took over the church
in 1637 for their services in French, which
continued until 1832. It was then leased
to the Church of the New Jerusalem, or
Swedenborgians. This denomination was
formed in 1787 by some followers of the
mystic Emmanuel Swedenborg. They
remained here until 1852, when they
moved to Park Lane.

In 1852, the church was leased to the
Catholic Apostolic Church, or Irvingites.
They were firm believers in the immanence

Opposite
(clockwise
from top left):
entrance from
Queen Street,
1938; interior,
looking west,
1938; south
chancel window
with piscina, in
1938; interior,
looking east, in
1938, when in use
by the Catholic
Apostolic Church

Below: exterior
from the south-
east in 1956, after
the demolition
of surrounding
buildings

Stranger connections

The church has had a chequered history, which includes a 300-year association with the Low Countries. Summed up in a sentence, it could be described as a minor medieval parish church, which was abandoned at the Reformation and passed into industrial use as a Strangers' cloth hall, and then became the Walloon Church. Today it is a Dutch, Flemish and Walloon history and study centre.

Current historical studies at St Mary-the-Less concern the influence of the Low Countries on East Anglian society and culture, with regard to migration, trade, architecture, weaving, printing, pottery, religion, land drainage, farming, horticulture, map-making, art, local dialect, place names and personal names. In Norfolk the principal places of settlement for migrants from the Netherlands were Norwich, Yarmouth, King's Lynn and Thetford. More contemporary activities at St Mary-the-Less include Dutch language teaching, translation, exhibitions and meetings about relations between Britain and the Low Countries.

A Low Countries library occupies the chancel of the church, and includes a collection of books, files and historical items. St Mary-the-Less is also used as the base of the Norfolk Strangers Association. The aims of the Association are the exchange of knowledge relating to the history of Dutch, Flemish, Walloon and Huguenot settlers and the effect of such settlement on the religious, economic and social life of Norfolk by means of research, lectures, visits to sites of interest and social gatherings. These activities are informed by a desire to perpetuate the memory of Stranger ancestors.

Dr William Woods, proprietor of the Dutch and Flemish Studies Centre, St Mary-the-Less

Left: the tower, viewed from Queen Street

Below: south porch from Queen Street today

(immediacy) of the Second Coming, and had no provision for continuing their ministry, and so as the ministers died, the denomination gradually dwindled. The Norwich minister died in 1953, and the church was given up. The church was then used as a parish hall for St Andrew's parish, and from 1959 until 1985 as a warehouse for Robertson & Coleman, a furnishing shop across the street.

The church is currently privately owned and in need of massive further work before it resumes a role in the community of the 21st century. Access is extremely difficult.

Top: interior of the chancel today

Above: the north door, with a carving marking 1637, the year the French-speaking Walloons took over the church

Right: tympanum of south door

St Michael Coslany (St Miles)

Oak Street, map reference C2

This elegant city-centre church dates from the
13th century but has been much rebuilt over the years.
It is particularly noted for its beautiful flushwork

Dedication The church is dedicated in honour of St Michael the Archangel, and in full to St Michael and All Angels. As with its neighbour St Mary, the suffix refers to the fact that it stands in the ward of Coslany. 'Miles' is a standard contraction of Michael, although it is never applied to the other four Michael churches in the city, of which two remain.

Exterior The church consists of nave, chancel, north aisle and chapel, south aisle and transept, and west tower. The church is noted for its remarkable display of flushwork – original 15th-century on the south aisle; on the chancel a remarkably good copy of 1884. The east window dates from this restoration, too, and the original was almost certainly much larger. The tower is tall and has been heightened, as the blocked lower belfry windows show.

The parapet has shields in lozenges. The west doors are medieval and traceried, and feature angels. This is one of the five towers of Norwich where bells are still rung, and St Michael's itself holds eight.

The church is known to have been in existence since 1284, although much rebuilt; some of this work has been ascribed to John Antell. It is possible to confirm the building dates of various parts of the church. The south aisle (and south porch, demolished in 1747) were added in 1500, by Alderman Gregory Clark; the chapel at its east end was added around the same time by Robert Thorpe, as his chantry chapel. The north aisle was built by Alderman William Ramsey in 1502–04. The nave was rebuilt in the early 16th century, by the Stalon brothers, who both held the office of sheriff. Unusually for an aisled church, there

Opposite: exterior from the east, showing the medieval flushwork on the south chapel and 19th-century copy on the chancel

Left: exterior from the south-east, painted by Sillett in the early 19th century, showing the blank east wall and chimney

Left: Victorian flushwork on the chancel

Opposite: detail from stained glass window showing the Deposition, in memory of Richard and Jane Bullard; interior of nave today, showing science centre activities

is no clerestory: one would have added more light. The huge Perpendicular windows are also a notable feature.

The whole building was thoroughly restored in 1883–4. The chancel was rebuilt and refaced, and a new east window inserted. The original one had been blocked up in 1741, and a vestry was later built against the east wall.

Interior Despite its piecemeal development, the interior of St Miles is an impressive space. It would have been divided up by screens in the Middle Ages: the rood screen across the chancel, and parclose screens cutting off the chapels. The arcade pillars are typical late Perpendicular in style. The font is a simple 14th-century design.

In 1741, the chancel was raised by three steps, and paved in white Portland stone "with black marble dotts at the corners". This floor was later relaid outside the west door, where it remains. Also at this time, a huge altar-piece was erected, which caused the east window to be blocked. It was 18 feet (5.5 metres) high, "divided into five parts … and curiously painted" (according to contemporary churchwardens' accounts). It was removed in the restoration of 1883, and is most probably the one now in St John Maddermarket, although its paintings are in Trowse church. At this time, the coloured shields were placed on the corbels, each bearing the attributed coat-of-arms of a saint.

Monuments There are several monuments. One, defaced, in the north chancel aisle, is probably that of William Ramsey, the builder of the north aisle.

General The major alteration after redundancy was the erection of the gallery and enclosed space under it at the west end, and the removal of all surviving fittings.

Furnishings moved elsewhere The church possessed an eagle lectern, presented in 1493 by William Westbrook. In 1776 it was sold to St Gregory Pottergate, where it remained until about 1974, when it was removed to St Giles (see page 49). The organ of 1883 was removed to Trinity URC on Unthank Road in 1979. Its predecessor, after several moves, is now at Calthorpe.

Above: medieval west door in 1938

Right: interior, looking west, 1938

Science for all ages

Three generations of us went to the Inspire Discovery Centre at St Michael Coslany for my partner's son's fourth birthday weekend. Our preschooler made slime, which he thought was great and got to bring away. Standing inside the giant bubble is definitely popular, as are the never-ending mirrors and the ball-sorter that can be filled and emptied over and over again to look at probabilities and distribution. He didn't want to leave, which is a real sign of success!

It's all hands-on, so everyone can have a go. And the range of exhibits is great and for all ages – we ALL played with them, grandparents included. They are well planned and rugged for inquisitive little hands.

We like the atmosphere – it's very relaxed, and there's lots to do and lots of space to run around! I think it's great the centre is based in a church; the space, particularly the height, gives it a different feel to other activity venues. The space is well used and the atmospheric architecture creates a discussion point.

Louise Bohn

St Michael-at-Plea

Queen Street, map reference D4

There has been a church on this site since Anglo-Saxon
times, and before that it was a pagan place of worship.
The clock face bears an unusual inscription

Dedication The church is dedicated
in honour of St Michael the Archangel.
The suffix 'at Plea' refers to the archdeacon's
court, which was held in the church.
It was also occasionally called St Michael
Motstow, because it was the meeting place
of the Norwich moot.

Exterior The church consists of nave,
chancel, north and south transepts, south
chapel, south porch and west tower. The
chancel is the earliest part, and is probably
of the 13th century. The nave, transepts
and chancel aisle were all built in the 15th
century. The tower is also 15th-century. Its
top storey was removed in the 18th century,
and a cupola placed on top to house the
bell. In the 1887 restoration the cupola
was removed, and the large pinnacles
added. The porch is faced with freestone,
with flushwork Ms (for Michael), and has
carvings of St Michael and the dragon in
its spandrels. The clock is well known in
Norwich for its 'forget-me-not' inscription.

Interior Most of the furnishings have
been removed, but there is a late medieval
font, with a fine 17th-century cover. The
original nave roof survives, with carved
angels. The oak screen was erected in 1908.
The church was reordered and restored in
1887. Until then, the seating for the court
remained in the chancel.

Monuments There is an interesting
monument to Jacques de Hem (d. 1603),
near the font.

General St Michael's is one of the earlier
church foundations in Norwich, and its
foundation is of Anglo-Saxon date. No trace
remains of the original church, which was
probably built in the 11th or 12th century.
Excavation has revealed that the site was
a pagan Anglo-Saxon cremation cemetery
of the fifth or sixth century, meaning that
this has been a religious site for more than
1,500 years. The church became redundant
in the 1960s, and is now in the care of the

Norwich Historic Churches Trust.

Furnishings moved elsewhere
Some very important late medieval
panel paintings are now in the Cathedral.
The organ is at Swanton Morley.

Opposite:
the tower
and outsized
pinnacles; the
interior today,
looking east.
Note how the
chancel 'weeps'
(leans) slightly
to the north

Above: exterior
from the south,
drawn by Sillett
in 1828, showing
the tower with
cupola before
the pinnacles
were added

Below: interior in
1937, before the
removal of the
rood and figures
from the screen

A popular meeting place

I originally ran the SPCK (Society for Promoting Christian Knowledge) shop in Pottergate, which moved to St Michael at Plea in 2004. SPCK invested a lot in the building, including completely limewashing it and putting in new fittings to make it welcoming and bright.

I took it over to run the Norwich Christian Resource Centre in 2008 and wanted to set up something that was more than just a shop, somewhere people could come and meet, with a cafeteria. We now hold talks and all sorts of events here, from wedding receptions to a medieval night. I want to get more young people involved, with young Christian musicians playing here, for example.

What struck me is what a beautiful and peaceful building it is. We get a lot of tourists and visitors who just want to look at the fabric of the building, and they are so pleased that all the memorials and gravestones are still available to look at. They come from all over, in particular Japan and America.

I'm happy, apart from the heating bill! Three industrial heaters have been installed and hang from the ceilings – they are normally used in aircraft hangars to keep aircraft warm, so they really do the trick.

Steve Foyster, manager and director of Norwich Christian Resource Centre

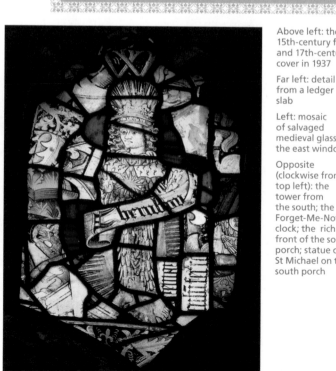

Above left: the 15th-century font and 17th-century cover in 1937

Far left: detail from a ledger slab

Left: mosaic of salvaged medieval glass in the east window

Opposite (clockwise from top left): the tower from the south; the Forget-Me-Not clock; the rich front of the south porch; statue of St Michael on the south porch

St Peter Hungate

Princes Street, map reference C4

St Peter's was once "one of the most fashionable places
of worship in Norwich", drawing huge congregations.
Since 2008 it has housed Hungate Medieval Art

Dedication The church is dedicated
in honour of St Peter the apostle. He is
supposed to have been crucified upside-
down; this would seem to be a pious myth,
although it explains why an inverted cross
is sometimes found as his emblem, either
with or instead of the crossed keys, which
is his other symbol.

Exterior The church consists of nave,
chancel, north and south transepts, south
porch, and west tower. The tower is square
and of black flint, built in 1431 by Thomas
Ingham. Its unusual pyramid cap was put
on in 1906, after the battlemented belfry
stage had become so unsafe that it was
taken down, possibly around 1888. The
south porch was added in 1497, by Nicholas
Ingham, who is buried in it. It has angle
buttresses and a niche for a statue over the
door. Its ceiling has four bosses – one for
each Evangelist. The nave and transepts
were totally rebuilt, as "a neat building
of black flint", by John and Margaret
Paston in 1458, after they had acquired the
advowson from St Mary's College. A stone
in a buttress near the north door records
this: it shows a tree trunk without branches
(representing the decay of the old church)
with a new shoot (the new building),
together with the date of completion,
1460. The nave and transept windows are
uniformly Perpendicular, and allow much
light into the building.

The chancel had been rebuilt in 1431
by Thomas Ingham and was rebuilt again
in 1604 after it collapsed. It is of rough
rubble, plastered over, and contrasts
strongly with the higher quality work of
the nave and transepts. Its windows are of
an older pattern with trefoil tracery in the
heads. It is covered with pin-tiles, which
date from the 1604 rebuilding.

Interior Both the north and the south
doors are original – of about 1460 – and
have tracery that is similar to that in the

windows. The nave has wall-arcading, to
frame each window. The nave roof is of low
pitch, and angels with scrolls adorn it. There
is a central boss, of Christ in Judgment. The
font is 15th-century, and its cover, with
an open-work steeple, is dated 1605.

There are two squints which give
a view from the nave into the transepts.
In the south transept is a niche which held
a statue of St John the Baptist, and John
Paston is buried in front of it, although
his grave is now unmarked. The headstops
on the window in the south transept are
supposed to represent him and his wife.
In the north transept the doors to the
rood-stair can be seen.

The collapse of the chancel in 1604
demolished the rood screen, and it was never
replaced. The east window is filled with
pieces of medieval glass. Blomefield, writing
in 1741, says that much of the original glass
survived in the chancel, but much was later
lost through neglect. What remains has been
assembled in this window.

The church was one of the earliest in
Norwich to be affected by the Oxford
Movement. The square pews were replaced
by chairs. Under William Hull, Rector
from 1871 until 1901, the services took on

Below: exterior
from the north,
showing the
original top of
the tower, as
drawn by Sillett
in 1828

Opposite: the
east window,
with medieval
glass, reset by
G King and Sons
in 1904

S. PETER, HUNGATE.

a very ritualistic character, with candles, incense and banners, and the church was "one of the most fashionable places of worship in Norwich", according to Hull's obituary which appeared in the *Daily Press* on 15 April 1901. Apparently the congregations were so large that the choir had to squeeze through them in single file. By the end of the century it was again in a bad way: in 1888, the tower was so dangerous that an order was served on the churchwardens. In 1897, a large hole in the chancel roof was covered only by a tarpaulin.

Although restored in 1906, the church was in bad state again by 1931, and was threatened with demolition. The Norfolk Archaeological Trust raised money to repair it, and it was used as a museum of church art from 1936 until 1995. It came under the care of the Norwich Historic Churches Trust in 2008, in which year Hungate Medieval Art was formed.

Monuments There is one monument: on the west wall, to Matthew Goss, who died in 1779.

William Bridge The notorious puritan William Bridge was rector of St Peter's, and its neighbour St George Tombland, until he was ejected and excommunicated in 1638, although he had abandoned both offices by

early 1637. He went to Rotterdam, where he became Minister of the English Church from 1638 to 1642. By his name in the list of such clergy Charles I wrote: "We are well rid of him". On his return to England he was Minister at Yarmouth until 1660, when he was again ejected. He then became Pastor of Yarmouth Congregational Church from 1643 until his death in 1670, and of the Old Meeting House Congregational Church in Colegate.

Top: exterior today, from the west, showing the lowered tower

Above left: the medieval font

Above right: the medieval north door

Hungate Medieval Art

Hungate Medieval Art opened to the public in April 2009. The project's founders had sought a sympathetic use for St Peter Hungate – a church of a manageable size, in a good location, which had always been very popular with visitors.

Having secured a lease from the Norwich Historic Churches Trust who own the building, fundraising was undertaken to complete some necessary restoration work. The walls of the church were limewashed, the stained glass was cleaned and a bell was added for disabled visitors.

Hungate Medieval Art aims to promote the medieval art and architecture of Norfolk. In particular, the charity is concerned with the medieval art in the county's parish churches.

The first of the centre's permanent exhibitions looks at stained glass in Norfolk. Beautiful backlit colour photographs highlight some of the glass which can still be seen in parish churches across the county, and a set of stained glass trails are available to help visitors explore them. On most Saturday mornings a team of stained glass conservators use the centre as a workshop, so visitors can watch them at work and learn more about the process.

The centre has also been very lucky to acquire some carved medieval pews from the church of St Andrew in Tottington. This church isn't open to the public because it is located in the Stanford Battle Area, so the pews came to Hungate so that more people ccould enjoy them.

Hungate has been really well received. It appeals to people with a variety of interests – history, craftsmanship, art and architecture. The goodwill of our visitors and a growing team of committed volunteers have helped to take the project forward.

Being based in a medieval church complements our exhibition and activities – St Peter Hungate has some high-quality glass from the 15th and 16th centuries, as well as some great examples of medieval carving and a stunning hammerbeam roof. In the future we're aiming to expand the exhibitions in the centre to showcase other medieval art forms too.

Dale Copley, centre manager,
Hungate Medieval Art

Above left: detail from the east window

Above: medieval benches from Tottington church

Left: interior of the nave, showing an exhibition of medieval stained glass

St Peter Mancroft

Millennium Plain, map reference E2

The architectural historian Pevsner remarked on the
extravagance of St Peter Mancroft's construction.
The church's east window contains the most extensive
collection of 15th-century Norwich glass

Dedication The church is in fact
dedicated in honour of St Peter and St Paul.
Peter is supposed to have been crucified
upside-down, but this would seem to be
a pious myth, although it explains why
an inverted cross is sometimes found as
his emblem, either with or instead of the
crossed keys, his other symbol. Paul is
supposed to have been martyred by being
beheaded with a sword, which has become
his symbol. Mancroft, a name frequently
said to derive from the Latin *magna crofta*
('great field') is more likely to come form
the Old English *gemæne croft*, meaning
'common field'. Both refer to the fact that
such a field stood to the south of the church
until quite late, and the college founded
across the street, on the site of the Assembly
House, was called St Mary-in-the-Field.

Exterior The church consists of nave,
chancel, north and south aisles and chapels,
north and south transepts, north and
south porches, and west tower. There is
also a three-storey east vestry. The whole
church is clad in freestone ashlar, which is
an indication of the wealth of the parish.
The present fabric dates from a major
rebuilding of 1430, which was completed
by 1455. The tower is very elaborate,
with panelling and image niches (which
seem never to have been occupied), and
Pevsner's assessment, that it is "more rich
than aesthetically successful" and that its
"prodigality has defeated its object", may
well stand. It certainly has something of
the wedding-cake about it. The parapet,
'pepperpot' pinnacles and flèche are all of
1895. The ground stage is open on the west,
north and south sides, to accommodate
a processional way. The corresponding
processional path under the east end was
blocked by construction of the coffee bar in
1983. The south porch is simpler than the
north, which faces the market, and this is
to be expected.

Interior This is a large, light interior,
undivided by screens. It is 180 feet (55
metres) long, and the clerestory, of 17
windows each side, is almost entirely glass.
It is roofed by a version of hammerbeam
construction, in which the hammerbeams
are hidden by coving. (The same version
occurs at St John Maddermarket.)

The furnishings all date from the
refitting of 1851. Of the medieval
fittings, the font is of 1463. It was a Seven
Sacrament font, but has been violently
mutilated. It was at one point removed,
and not reinstated until 1926. Its canopy,
although reproducing the medieval
appearance (except for the paint), is largely
a Victorian reconstruction of 1887, which
used what original material was left. There
is a similar one at Trunch.

The reredos is of 1886 by JW Seddon,
but Ninian Comper added the lower row
of figures (Saints Alban, Augustine of
Canterbury, Columba and Felix) and
gilded it, in 1930.

There are two organs, one at the east
end, built by Renatus Harris in 1707 but
much altered, and one at the west end,
by Peter Collins, installed in 1984.

Opposite: the
tower, seen from
the market.
Crenellations,
pinnacles and
flèche all date
from 1895

Below: exterior
from the south in
the 19th century

The east window contains the most extensive collection of Norwich glass. It is of 15th-century date, with 42 panels containing the stories of Christ, the Virgin, St Peter and John the Evangelist.

Monuments As befits a church of this social importance, there are many important and interesting monuments. One of the principal ones commemorates Thomas Browne (d. 1682), physician and author.

General St Peter Mancroft was founded in 1075 by Ralph de Guader, Earl of Norfolk. Little is known about its original structure, as it was almost completely rebuilt in the 15th century. It is thought that the original church was cruciform, with a central tower. In the late 14th century, a piecemeal redevelopment of the church began with the building of a new tower to the west of the church. This tower may have been designed to be freestanding but, as the chancel and nave were redesigned, the tower became incorporated into the church.

Mancroft claims to have been the first place in the world to have rung a true peal of bells. Recorded on 2 May 1715, the Norwich Scholars rang Mancroft's 13 bells, changing their order more than 5,000 times without repetition. A plaque in the church commemorates the feat.

ST PETER'S MANCROFT CHURCH.

Left: interior, looking east, 1849

Below left: the tower, showing the processional way through it

Below right: view into the south transept. The screen is part of the old organ case

Left: detail of a monument to Francis Wyndham (d. 1592)

Above: the Jesus Chapel in the north choir aisle

Sir Thomas Browne

Browne was born in 1605 in London, but studied at Oxford University in what is now Pembroke College. He then took medical courses at universities in Montpellier, France; Padua, Italy; and Leiden, Holland, obtaining his MD. After practice in London he moved in 1636 to Norwich, where he remained for the rest of his life. He was elected a Fellow of the Royal College of Physicians of London, the oldest medical college in England, in 1664. He wrote extensive treatises on philosophical topics, including *Religio Medici* (1643) and *Pseudodoxia Epidemica* (1646).

Charles II, after his restoration in 1660, visited Norwich and knighted Browne in Blackfriars Hall in 1671, probably because he was true to the Royalist cause and because of his medical eminence. (In those days physicians knew everything and did nothing – they would not even touch the patient, let alone cut or stitch them. That was left to the surgeons – a lesser breed!)

Browne lived in a house in Orford Place, which has since been demolished. In 1641 he married Dorothy Mileham of Burlingham, Norfolk, and they had 12 children. He died in 1682 and was buried in St Peter Mancroft, where Lady Dorothy was also buried three years later.

He is remembered on account of his erudite writings, which were highly respected by scholars down the centuries. He is a great Norvicensian and someone of whom the city is justifiably proud. In 2005 Dr Batty Shaw, who organised the 300th anniversary celebrations of Browne's death in 1982, asked the Norwich Medicochirurgical Society (the oldest medical society in England) to help organise the 400th anniversary of his birth. With the help of Professor Richard Ball and Dr Robert Jarvis, I organised a two-day symposium where eminent Browne scholars read papers about various aspects of his work. There was also a concert at Norwich Cathedral with music and Browne readings, a fascinating tour of Browne's Norwich and a service of thanksgiving in St Peter Mancroft.

Barry Ross, MB FRCS, retired surgeon and member of the Norwich Medicochirurgical Society

Above: detail of
the east window
(1921) in the
south chapel, by
Herbert Hendrie

Right: the
clerestory and
roof

Top right: statue of St Peter on the quire stalls

Above: statue of the Blessed Virgin Mary and Child

Left: interior today, looking west

St Peter Parmentergate

King Street, map reference E4

This church, built on a historic route through the city, houses the magnificent tomb of Richard Berney and his wife, which dates from 1623

Dedication The church is dedicated in honour of St Peter, one of the apostles. He is supposed to have been crucified upside-down, but this would seem to be a pious myth. However, it explains why an inverted cross is sometimes found as his emblem, either with or instead of the crossed keys, his other symbol. 'Parmentergate' means the street of the parmenters: leatherworkers or parchment makers. This has now become Mountergate, and a false form, St Peter per Mountergate (that is, by Mountergate), grew up as a result. Early documents refer to the church as Parmentergate or Parmenterstrete.

Exterior The church consists of nave, chancel, south porch and west tower. There is also an east vestry. Built on a slope, the church is notable for its great height. The glorious tower, with its double crenellated parapet and richly moulded openings, is best viewed from the south-west. The windows are uniform on both sides of the church. They are in the Perpendicular style, dating from the 15th century – the nave was rebuilt between 1475 and 1500. The absence of any cusping in the tracery suggests a no-frills building budget. The chancel is a little later, between 1500 and 1525. The two-storey south porch, of the same date as the chancel, is plain with uncarved shields in the door spandrels.

Over the west door there are shields, commemorating the families who paid for the rebuilding of the church. The shields in the spandrels, featuring St Peter with a model of the church, and a woman with a rosary, are both Victorian copies.

On the north side the doorway has been blocked. The turret houses stairs to the former rood loft. It blocks off part of a window, suggesting it was either a later addition or has been radically altered.

The two-storey vestry was built in 1511. Its entrance was originally to the south of the altar, but the erection of the Berney monument caused it to be moved to the north side. It may be compared with the rather grander three-storey vestry at St Peter Mancroft.

Interior The inside of the building is lofty but plain, a sign again of a limited building budget. The nave walls do not have wall arches and the low-pitched nave roof is of simple construction. The elegant chancel arch makes a successful transition to the more steeply roofed chancel. The doorway to the rood loft stair is in the north wall of the nave.

Of the furnishings, all that remains are the font, screen and chancel stalls. The font is contemporary with the rebuilding. The font pedestal, which features woodwoses ('wild men') alternating with lions, is notable because unusually one of the two woodwoses is a woman. The screen, of which only the dado survives, is medieval on the north side; the south side is a good 19th-century reproduction. The stalls, erected for the college of priests that was once situated to the north of the church, are partially original. There are 24 in total, of which 16 are medieval. The panel tracery of the 14th century implies that they must

Below: exterior from the north-east (undated)

Opposite: the tower from the west

Life goes forward

I was born in 1926 in St Julian's Street, Norwich and was a member of the congregation until I was 28, when I married and moved to Taverham, where I've lived ever since.

St Peter Parmentergate was an Anglo-Catholic church. There was mass every day at 7 o'clock in the morning, so many people went before starting work at 8 o'clock. I was a regular attendee and didn't miss mass on a Sunday in 28 years unless I was ill. I used to go with my three brothers who are all older than me. It's a big church and there was quite a lot going on, and it was always well-attended, with a lot of children.

I went back about 20 years ago and was horrified at all the dust that was there and at how different it looked. I don't like to think about the church where I used to worship not being used for that anymore, but there are a lot of churches around and they are not full, so I think having a martial arts centre here is a reasonable outcome for a redundant church. Life goes forward and it's nice to see the church being used by young people.

Rosemary Frost

Above: interior, looking east, 1937

Below left: Berney monument of 1623, photographed in 1937

Below right: south side exterior, looking west

pre-date the chancel. During the 19th-century restoration, acoustic jars (used to improve the resonance of the building) were found in the chancel floor.

The reredos was installed in 1889, and given by the vicar, William Hudson, in memory of his wife. The upper part contains shields of the demolished churches subsumed into the parish: John the Evangelist, Michael Conesford and Vedast, and Francis (commemorating the Greyfriars' convent).

Monuments By the site of the altar stands the tomb of Richard Berney and his wife Elizabeth (née Hobart), erected in 1623 by Elizabeth's father Edward Hobart. Its stiff recumbent figures under an elaborate Jacobean canopy alone make the church worth a visit. It is of plaster on a wooden frame, and the iconography is rather more pre- than post-Renaissance. Allegorical figures of Faith, Hope, and Charity stand on the canopy, together with Time. It was extensively repaired in late 2008.

General The original building, probably small and in the Norman style, was presented by Roger Bigod to the Cathedral Priory in the late 11th century. In the late 15th and early 16th centuries it was completely rebuilt, financed by the prosperity of its location on a main route through the city,

close to the merchants' quays.

The church was thoroughly restored, in line with ecclesiological principles, in 1861 and 1867. It was declared redundant in 1981, when the congregation decided to move to St John Timberhill and make that the parish church of the united parish of Parmentergate.

In 2005, after being empty for some time, the main church building became the Norwich Centre for Martial Arts. The vestry houses the office of Norwich Historic Churches Trust.

Furnishings moved elsewhere The organ was broken up, and parts of it are in the instrument in Norwich School chapel.

Top: interior today, looking east. The removal of the pews allows the church's proportions to be appreciated

Above: the 19th-century reredos

St Saviour

Magdalen Street, map reference B3

Now in use as a youth theatre, St Saviour's was the incumbency of Harris Cooke from 1856. The vicar's faithful congregation persuaded him to stay for 53 years, despite several offers of livings from other parishes

Dedication There was no saint called 'Saviour'. The church is dedicated in honour of 'the Transfiguration of the Holy Saviour', and so for convenience the name was cut down.

Exterior The church consists of nave, chancel, south porch and west tower. The tower has an odd appearance, explained by the fact that its top storey was removed in 1853, when a new set of battlements was built. The belfry windows were reset lower down on the north and south sides, while on the west face the sound-hole was left in place instead. The west doorway was remodelled, either at this time or possibly when the south porch was rebuilt in 1728. The original 15th-century doorway has been reset and much mutilated.

The nave was restored in 1852, but retains its Perpendicular windows. Those in the chancel have reticulated tracery, and are of the 14th century; the chancel itself was restored in 1923.

Interior The furnishings, which were simple and largely dated from the 1852 restoration, have all been removed. Of these, the font is now in St George Colegate. It consists of an octagonal bowl with quatrefoils set on a shaft with engaged shafts, grotesque heads at the bases, and nodding ogees above. The bowl and shaft are clearly from two different fonts, but which was the original St Saviour's font? The gallery, a wooden Gothic erection, is now in All Saints, in a reduced form. The Commandment Boards behind the altar, pitch-pine pews, and an organ of 1860 in the gallery were still in place when the church

S.ͭ SAVIOUR, S.W.

Opposite: exterior from the south-west, showing the truncated tower

Left: exterior from the south-west, showing the original tower height, drawn by Sillett in 1828

Clockwise from above: exterior from the south-west in 1939, before the removal of the railings and construction of the flyover; interior view, looking east, 1938; postcard of the interior c. 1910; interior, looking west, 1938

A church with character

The notorious film *A Clockwork Orange*, released in 1971, showed a bleak future in a concrete city. In the same year Magdalen Street in Norwich was carved in two by a new flyover, and nearly 40 years later the space immediately around it remains very bleak. This is the setting of St Saviour's church – but, in spite of its oppressive neighbour, the small church is cheeky and very likeable. It is also full of fun inside. Because it's used by young people, however, it is usually only accessible to visitors by arrangement or on Heritage Open Days.

1971 was also the year in which the Friends of Norwich Churches was formed to help St Saviour's and other churches facing redundancy. As a result of their work, the city was soon able to set up the Norwich Historic Churches Trust, which now cares for 18 of the medieval churches.

Michael Wingate, Surveyor of the Fabric, Norwich Historic Churches Trust

was closed, but have long since disappeared. Their conservative nature is explained by the long incumbency of Harris Cooke, from 1856 until 1909. He was offered at least six other livings during this time, and each time refused, owing to pressure from his congregation at St Saviour.

The nave roof is concealed by a ceiling of plaster; the chancel roof dates from 1923.

After its closure, the church became first a parish hall, and then a badminton court. It is now in use as a youth centre and has been altered accordingly (not least the dark green and terracotta painted interiors) which makes appreciation of the building difficult.

Furnishings moved elsewhere The organ is now at Chippenham.

Top right and above: details of 19th-century stained glass in the church

Right: exterior from Magdalen Street

St Simon and St Jude

Elm Hill, map reference C4

This church was well attended until the late 19th century, when it fell into decline. Saved from demolition by the Norwich Society, it contains several remarkable monuments to the Pettus family, who lived on nearby Elm Hill

Dedication Simon and Jude are two of the apostles. Simon is occasionally known as Simeon Zelotes; Jude is sometimes called Thaddeus. Beyond what is related of them in the gospels, nothing is known about them, although legend says that they preached in Persia and were martyred there. Simon's symbol is a boat or fish, or occasionally a falchion (curved sword), with which he is supposed to have been hacked to pieces; Jude's is a club, also the instrument of his death, or a boat.

Exterior The church consists of nave, chancel and west tower. The tower partially fell in 1911 and remains as a jagged stump. The nave was built in 1415, and the chancel a little earlier. The flintwork on the south nave wall is of very high quality. The east window is a 16th- or 17th-century replacement of the Decorated original, but without the tracery's finer points. The basic outline, as left here, ties up with the tracery of the windows in the south walk of the Cathedral cloister, which date from the 1320s.

Interior Nothing remains of the furnishings. The nave is divided horizontally by a concrete floor inserted in the 1950s. The chancel, which had been divided up into a warren of small rooms, was cleared out and restored in 2008. The west gallery remains, incorporated into the later work. Early photographs of around 1900 show that it retained its box-pews – those in the chancel facing west – and that there was a standard Classical-style reredos, with semi-circular communion rails.

Monuments On either side of the chancel arch are the Pettus monuments. The Pettus family had a house on Elm Hill. To the south of the arch is Thomas (d. 1597), and his wife and sons. He was mayor of Norwich in 1590. To the north is John (d. 1614), with two sons and a daughter; he was mayor in 1608. On the same monument is Augustus (d. 1613) and his wife and son. The monuments were conserved in 2008.

General The church was very well attended until about 1870, when it seems to have gone into decline, and was eventually declared redundant in 1892. The parish was united with St George Tombland in 1894. After redundancy it was used as a Sunday School until 1918, and then gradually fell into decay. It was saved from demolition by the Norwich Society.

Furnishings moved elsewhere The altar table is in the Lady chapel in St George Tombland. The organ of 1887 went to Scarning; its predecessor is at Sidestrand.

Below: exterior from the north-east, showing the tower before its collapse, drawn by Sillett in 1828

Opposite: exterior of the south side

ST SIMON, and JUDE.

Clockwise from top left: interior, looking west, 1938; exterior in 1938, the church almost obliterated by ivy; interior looking east, 1938; the east window today

Top left: plaque depicting Sir Thomas Pettus and his wife, Christian Dethick, who died at the end of the 16th century

Top right: monument to Sir John Pettus (Mayor of Norwich 1608–9) and his wife, Bridget Curtis

Right: the ruin of the tower with the stair turret

St Stephen

Rampant Horse Street, map reference E3

An oasis of calm next to the bustling Chapelfield
shopping centre, St Stephen's retains a number of medieval
furnishings. The east window features five large figures
in stained glass, brought over from Germany in 1511

Dedication Stephen was a deacon in the early church in Jerusalem. The story of his martyrdom (by stoning to death) is told in the Acts of the Apostles, chapters 6 and 7.

Exterior The church consists of nave, chancel, north and south aisles and chapels, and north porch, which forms the base of the tower. There appears to have been a west tower, which was demolished to make way for the grand west end with its large window. Unusually, the nave and chancel post-date the aisles that surround them, which are of about 1350. The chancel was reconstructed between 1521 and 1534, and the nave between 1533 and 1550, which makes it post-Reformation. The clerestory is of 1540, and Renaissance motifs can be seen in the columns that separate the windows. The north porch is 1350, and was raised to form a tower in 1601 (the date used to be on the outside in iron figures, but they were removed). Again, the transition from Gothic to Renaissance can be seen as the tower rises. The porch vault contains two bosses, of St Stephen and of St Lawrence, another deacon martyr.

Interior The interior is no longer divided by its screens, and so the space can be appreciated. The change in decoration between the chancel (pre-Reformation) and the nave (post-Reformation) is very apparent. The arcade piers, although they appear to be Perpendicular, are in fact early Renaissance in style. The roof is a hammerbeam construction. Piscinae for the altars of the Lady chapel (north-east) and St Mary Magdalen chapel (south-east) remain.

Medieval furnishings include four stalls with misericords in the chancel, and the font, which is 16th century, with a 17th-century cover. The font now stands in the transept (once the chapel of St Anne). Just to the south of the transept, stencilling on the ceiling with the letter T indicates the site of the chapel of St Thomas.

Otherwise the furnishings mostly date from the 1859 refitting by Phipson. The reredos was installed in 1894, and consists of painting on zinc panels, executed by Lucy Bignold. It contains the Ten Commandments, the Creed and the Lord's Prayer, and is a very old-fashioned style of reredos for this date.

The glass in the east window has five large figures of 1511, which were brought here from the Mariawald monastery on the Ruhr; the rest, however, is a jigsaw of pieces assembled from what was left after the 'Great Blow' of 1648, when an arsenal blew up in Bethel Street, shattering glass in all the nearby buildings.

Monuments Of note is the brass to Thomas Cappe, vicar 1530–45, who rebuilt the chancel. It shows him wearing albe and cope (ecclesiastical garments), and is in the

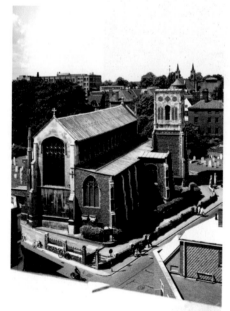

Opposite: detail of stained glass in the south aisle, 1904

Left: exterior from the north-east, 1962

Left: detail of window in the north transept

Above: detail of a misericord

Below left: the nave arcade

Opposite: exterior from the north (note the change from medieval to Renaissance style as the tower rises); interior, looking west

sanctuary. The monument to Elizabeth Coppin, in the south aisle, although a fairly ordinary composition, is interesting as it is made of coade, an artificial stone.

General The south-east chapel was enclosed by wood and glass screens to form a meeting room. Since the opening of Chapelfield shopping centre, the churchyard has become a busy throughway, and the west doors were replaced by glass ones in 2007 to allow the inside of the church to be seen even when it is closed.

Furnishing moved elsewhere The original organ of 1808 went in 1880 to Cawston, where it remains.

A welcoming tradition

St Stephen's has a long history of being welcoming and forward-thinking. In the 1500s a vicar based here embraced the Reformation and new ways of thinking, such as the movement to make scriptures accessible to people in the pews.

Today, the way the congregation has embraced the new Chapelfield shopping centre development next door continues this tradition. Historically there's always been a path through the churchyard (previously it went to the St Peter Mancroft vicarage), but the congregation took a lot of stick from the public when the path was reopened to what is now Chapelfield. The upshot has been the opening up and relandscaping of the churchyard, and around 50,000 people now walk past the church each day. The congregation doubled during 2008–09, which I attribute to the church's location and the fact that it's serving the community and engaging with real people. The church has always mirrored what's happening in society in general, and we're keen to keep appealing to people in the local community.

In 2009 we noticed a crack in the east end wall and notified an engineer, who said it was moving significantly. The damage was caused by a burst water main underneath the church, so we've had to close the building while extensive structural repairs are carried out. We've had to take out the stained glass window while the east wall is underpinned. Specialist glaziers have told us the window needs to be restored, so we're now fundraising.

The Reverend Madeline Light, priest-in-charge

St Swithin

St Benedict's Street, map reference C1

St Swithin's name suggests it may date from Anglo-Saxon times. The church was completely rebuilt in the 15th century and the parish remained affluent for the next three centuries. Since 1980 it has been the home of Norwich Arts Centre

Dedication The church is dedicated in honour of St Swithin, Bishop of Winchester, who died in 862. The well-known legend attached to his name states that if it rains on his feast day (2 July) it will rain for a further 40 days. This dedication may well indicate an Anglo-Saxon foundation date.

Exterior The church consists of nave, chancel, and north and south aisles and chapels. The church appears very odd from outside, as there is no tower and no obvious entrance. The tower became unsafe and was demolished in 1882. It was replaced by the turret. There were porches either side of it, as at St Gregory's; entrance was through the west door. The original church was probably no longer than the one we see today, and its development has been restricted by its site. The windows are of the Decorated style, though those in the clerestory are square-headed Perpendicular. They show that it is a building of four bays, with no separate chancel. The rood-stair turret on the north side shows the original screen crossed halfway along, giving a chancel and nave of two bays each. Also on the north side is the Mission Hall, the result of a generous benefaction, built in 1908 and as large again as the church itself.

Interior Very little remains to be seen. Entry from Norwich Arts Centre is now through the east wall, where the altar once stood. Of special note are the arcades. That on the north (left as you enter) is a standard Perpendicular structure, with Gothic columns and arches; that on the south was remodelled around 1700 in the Classical style, with square piers and round arches.

All the fittings have been removed. They included an East Anglian 'lion' font, a screen of 1905 that separated off the altar (featuring a projection screen that could be raised and lowered for 'magic lantern' lectures), and an organ.

Monuments Anne Scottowe (d. 1650), William Willcocks (d. 1770), Catherine Suckling (mother of Horatio Nelson, d. 1767) and Abraham Robertson (d. 1777).

General In the 15th century the parish was rich enough to rebuild the church as it stands, and still contained some well-to-do parishioners in the 18th century. But by the 19th century the parish had become a slum. The church closed in 1881, reopened in 1883, then closed again in 1891 and fell into disrepair. It was thoroughly restored in 1905. Although the Mission Hall was the social centre of the parish, falling numbers of residents forced the church's final closure in 1951. After many years' use as a furniture store, it became the Norwich Arts Centre in 1980. The church is now used as the auditorium and the Mission Hall contains the restaurant, galleries and offices.

Furnishings moved elsewhere The organ is at Heckingham.

Below: exterior from the south, showing the tower before demolition, drawn by Sillett in 1828

Opposite: exterior from south (St Benedict's Street); interior, during a performance

Above: medieval misericords, photographed in 1938

Left: interior, looking west, in 1938, showing the 'classical' arcade

Below: the roof in 1938

Norwich Arts Centre

I've been going to the Norwich Arts Centre at St Swithin since 1994. I've seen people like Damien Rice, the Divine Comedy, Martha Wainwright, Coldplay (back in their early years), a former Norwich band called Cord and my brother-in-law's band. Nirvana played in 1989 but mum and dad would've flattened me if I'd have gone to that! I've also hosted events there, like The Next Big Thing talent competition, when I worked at the *Eastern Daily Press*.

Norwich Arts Centre is well respected as a venue across the UK. It works well as a venue for up-and-coming bands and for critically acclaimed acts who won't necessarily sell many albums but have very loyal underground fans.

Bands seem to like the fact that it's based in a church and often talk about it – when I saw Aqualung they said the last time they had been in a church was when they sang in the school choir! I think the acoustics are quite good and I like its bohemian characteristics and its lovely, intimate atmosphere.

David Helsdon, music fan

Top: exterior today, showing the new lobby at the east end of the church. The tower of St Margaret is visible beyond

Above: exterior from the south, in 1937

Right: the auditorium of Norwich Arts Centre

Lost churches

As well as the 31 medieval churches still standing in Norwich, there are almost as many that have been lost or ruined. Many were demolished after the Reformation, for others very little information remains. Some churches survived until the last century, when they were destroyed in World War II bombing raids on the city and never rebuilt. This chapter looks at six lost churches, for which there is plenty of documentary and photographic evidence available, and at 22 further churches, about which much less is known.

St. Bartholomew's Church

The remains of the 14th century church, the building was desecrated in 1549.

St Bartholomew

Ber Street, map reference F4

Dedication Bartholomew was one of the apostles. The name means 'son of Tolmai', but he is occasionally called Nathanael in the gospels. He is traditionally supposed to have been martyred in Armenia, by being flayed alive.

Exterior The church appears to have consisted of an aisleless nave and chancel with a square west tower, and to have been built of flint with freestone dressings. The nave was 51 feet (15.5 metres) long and the chancel 15 feet (4.6 metres) long, according to measurements made by Messent; they were both 16 feet (4.9 metres) wide.

General The church was declared redundant in 1549, but appears not to have been demolished. The parish was united with St John-de-Sepulchre. Substantial remains, incorporated in later buildings, stood as late as 1939, when they were measured by Messent and photographed by Plunkett. Following bomb damage to the east side of the street, what was left was demolished in the 1950s, apart from part of the south and west walls of the tower, which remain.

Top and right: St Bartholomew's remains, photographed by Plunkett in 1939

Above: the south doorway arch in 1965

Left: the remains of the tower of St Bartholomew today, on Ber Street (on the corner of Horn's Lane)

St Benedict

St Benedict's Street, map reference C1

Dedication Benedict (*c.* 480–*c.* 550) is credited with compiling the monastic Rule that bears his name, although in fact it incorporates ideas from earlier monastic leaders. He had monasteries at Subiaco and later at Monte Cassino.

Exterior As it stood before bombing, the church was of 15th-century date, and consisted of a clerestoried nave with north aisle (*c.* 1484), north and south porches, a chancel, and a round west tower with a 14th-century octagonal belfry.

Interior The church was noted for having replaced two of its three arcade piers with cast iron columns during the 19th century – apparently to improve the sight-lines for those sitting in the aisle. There was a 15th-century font, which is now at Erpingham. The other furnishings, which dated from the 1899 refitting, were all destroyed.

General Archaeological work on the site in 1972 revealed four building phases, and identified the earliest church as 11th century, consisting of nave and apsidal chancel. Three burials which pre-dated this church were discovered, implying that an earlier church, probably wooden, stood on the site.

The church was so dilapidated in 1860 that serious consideration was given to demolishing it and building a new one. It was restored in that year: the east wall was rebuilt, a new east window inserted, and the lead roof replaced by slates. It was again restored in 1899. The church was gutted by incendiary bombs in 1942. The remains were demolished except for the tower, which still stands. As with St Andrew and St Peter Mancroft, the parishioners held the advowson, and appointed by preaching contest.

Top left: exterior from the south, 1934

Bottom left: interior, looking east, 1938

Below: the tower, with 14th-century belfry stage

St Crowches

Exchange Street, map reference D3

Dedication As with St Saviour, there was no saint called 'Crowches'. The word is a corruption of the Latin *crucis*, meaning cross, and in other places there are churches called St Cross. The dedication is thus in honour of the Holy Cross.

General The church was declared redundant in 1551 and it was assumed that it had been demolished. However, in 1838, when the Hole-in-the-Wall public house was being taken down to allow for the construction of Exchange Street, it was discovered that the pub was contained in the chancel of the church.

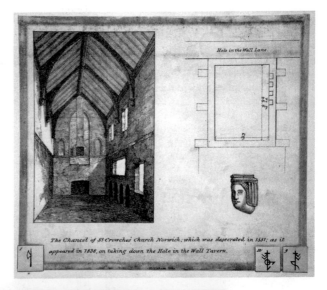

The Chancel of St Crowches Church Norwich; which was desecrated in 1551; as it appeared in 1838, on taking down the Hole in the Wall Tavern.

Above: drawing of surviving chancel by Henry Ninham (1838), looking east. Note the blocked window

Left: stone corbel, possibly the one in Ninham's sketch, in a nearby wall on St Andrew's Street (photographed in 1967)

St Michael-at-Thorn

Ber Street, map reference F4 (approximate)

Dedication The church was dedicated in honour of the archangel. The suffix referred to the fact that from an early date, the churchyard contained several thorn trees. The church was also known as St Michael-super-Montem, or St Miles-on-the-Hill.

Exterior The church originally consisted of a nave and chancel with no internal division, but with differing roofs, a square unbuttressed west tower and a south porch, all of around 1430. The tower fell in 1886 and was rebuilt in 1887; it had a distinctive crow-stepped parapet. A north aisle was added in 1836, and rebuilt in 1874. There was also a south transept, which appears in several drawings, but the date of its demolition (and, indeed, erection) is unclear.

Interior The church was refitted in the 1870s, in the usual ecclesiological manner with east-facing benches. A rood screen and reredos were later additions.

General St Michael-at-Thorn was one of the Ritualist churches, although it seems not to have attracted the unwelcome attention that its neighbour St John Timberhill did.

The church was gutted by incendiary bombs in 1942, and demolished 10 years later; the site is now a car park. All that remains is the Norman south door, which now forms the doorway to the cell at the rebuilt St Julian's.

Top right: exterior from the south, 1938

Above: interior, looking east, 1937

Left: south door of the nave in 1952, showing bomb damage. It is now at St Julian

St Paul

Barrack Street, map reference B4 (approximate)

Dedication Dedications to Paul the Apostle without Peter were very rare in the Middle Ages (apart from St Paul's Cathedral), but it is possible that he was the patron of this church. Other writers say it was Paul the Hermit (or Paul of Thebes), who died around 345. He is held to be the first Christian hermit, and to have lived in the Egyptian desert, dying at the age of more than a hundred. There is a faint possibility it was a double dedication, in honour of both saints.

Exterior The church consisted of nave and chancel with no structural division, north aisle and chapel, south porch, round west tower, and an eastern polygonal apse, which was added in 1870 to serve as a chancel. The tower had a late medieval octagonal belfry, but this was removed

in 1819. The building was mainly late 15th-century, and photographs show the windows were in the Perpendicular style.

Interior The church was refitted in the usual ecclesiological style in the later 19th century, probably at the same time as the apse was added. There was a 15th-century screen in the east bay of the arcade, separating the Lady Chapel, and part of it had been used to form a screen in the tower arch.

General The church also served Norman's Spital, a hospital founded between 1118 and 1145 and dissolved in 1534. After the Reformation St Paul's subsumed the parishes of the redundant churches of All Saints Fybriggate and St Margaret Combust.

Right: exterior from the north-west, 1932

Below: interior, looking east, in 1938, showing the 1870 apse (notice screen in east bay)

Below: drawing of the 15th-century chapel screen by Cotman (1817)

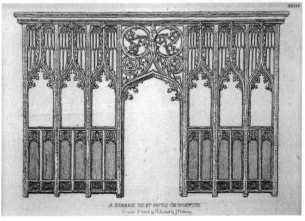

143

St Peter Southgate

Southgate Lane, map reference G5 (approximate)

Dedication This was the fourth Norwich church dedicated in honour of Peter the Apostle, appropriately, as fishermen probably formed the major part of the parish's population.

Exterior The church consisted of nave, chancel, north transept (of 1518) and west tower. The picture shows that the nave had one Decorated window of two lights, and one square-headed Perpendicular one of three lights; those in the chancel are less easy to read.

The tower had no buttresses, but the stair turret was very prominent. The building seems to have retained its external plaster, which covered all churches built of unfaced flint rubble; the plaster's removal was a Victorian obsession.

Interior The interior was never reordered, and retained its gallery and box-pews until the end.

General The church was in use until 1884, when the parish was united with St Etheldreda (the two parishes had had the same clergyman since 1822), and St Peter's was demolished, except for part of the tower. There is a green plaque on the wall nearby which, inaccurately, states that the church was demolished in 1387. The churchyard is now a playground.

ST PETER, SOUTHGATE.

St Peter Southgate, Norwich

Top: As drawn by Sillett, 1828

Above: exterior from south, c. 1869

Left: remains of the tower today

Churches lost before 1600

All Saints Fyebriggate The church stood on the west of Magdalen Street and on the north of Cowgate. It was demolished in 1550, although it had been sold off in two lots, the nave going to one purchaser, the chancel to another.

St Botolph Botolph was the Anglo-Saxon Abbot of Icanhoe, probably modern Iken. In towns, his churches often stood near gateways, and the boundary of the Saxon town was indeed just north of the church (it was moved further north, to Magdalen Gate, in the later Middle Ages). The church stood in Botolph Street, now under Anglia Square in Magdalen Street. It was demolished in 1548.

St Catherine Newgate The church was actually dedicated in honour of St Wynwaloe, a Breton abbot, but in popular usage the dedication was changed on account of a wonder-working statue of St Catherine of Alexandria that was in it. The church stood near the junction of Surrey Street and Queen's Road, on the site of Notre Dame convent. Some reused blocks of freestone may be seen in the walls. The parish was united with All Saints Westlegate.

St Christopher This church stood on the south side of Princes Street, between the junction with Elm Hill and St Andrew's Plain. It was burnt in 1507, and not replaced. The parish was united with St Andrew.

St Clement-at-the-Well The dedication to St Clement of Rome (as St Clement-at-Fyebridge) may indicate Danish activity in this part of the town. It was also known as St Clement Conesford. The church stood on the east side of King Street, opposite the junction with Music House Lane, on the site of the Waterfront. The parish was united with St Julian. It was largely demolished in 1560, although a significant amount of the fabric stood until about 1829, incorporated into other buildings.

St Cuthbert Cuthbert is the great saint of Northumbria, who died in 687, and it is unclear why he should have a church dedication in East Anglia. There is one other pre-Reformation dedication in the county, at Thetford, and both churches stand to the south of the marketplaces. The parish was united with St Mary-the-Less, and the church was demolished in 1535. It stood on the east side of Upper King Street, where its approximate site is commemorated by St Cuthbert's House. It may be possible to trace the outline of the churchyard in the property boundaries.

St Edward the Martyr Edward was King of England 975–979, when he was assassinated at Corfe as a result of a political power struggle. Following miracles at his grave, he was translated to Shaftesbury. There were five pre-Reformation churches dedicated in his honour. The church stood very close to the west of St Etheldreda in King Street, and was probably across Argyle Street. In 1269 it was attached to a hospital known as Hildebrond's or Ivyhall, and was demolished in 1540, although Blomefield said that remains were still to be seen in 1738. The parish was united with St Julian.

St Ethelbert There are two saints called Ethelbert – this church was dedicated in honour of the king of East Anglia, who was killed in 794 for political reasons by Offa of Mercia. He is the patron saint of Hereford Cathedral, as he met his death in that region. There were 11 churches dedicated in his honour in East Anglia. St Ethelbert's stood within what is now the Close, immediately to the south of the Ethelbert Gate on Almary Green. Parchmarks in the grass have confirmed this. The church was burnt in the 1272 riot and not rebuilt, but replaced by a chapel over the Ethelbert Gate.

St John Colegate Dedicated in honour of the Baptist. The church stood on the north side of Colegate, approximately on the site of the Octagon Chapel. It was subsumed into the first Blackfriars site in 1226, and ceased to be parochial; the parish was united with St George Colegate. After the friars moved to their new site over the river, in 1307, the church was kept up as an anchorhold. It was demolished in 1540.

St John the Evangelist The only John church in Norwich not dedicated in honour of the Baptist, it stood at the junction of Rose Lane and King Street. It was subsumed

145

into the Greyfriars site around 1300, and ceased to be parochial, the parish being incorporated into St Peter Parmentergate; the church was used as an anchorhold. It was demolished in about 1534.

St Margaret Combust Dedicated in honour of the mythical St Margaret of Antioch (see St Margaret-de-Westwick, p80). For the suffix 'Combust', see St Mary Unbrent. Also known as St Margaret Fybriggate, the church stood at the north end of Magdalen Street, on the west side, about 100 yards south of the remains of the city wall. It was demolished in 1547, and the parish united with St Paul. Archaeological work in 1987 uncovered what was probably the base of the east wall, and many burials. This confirmed the church's somewhat grisly alternative name, *Sancta Margareta ubi sepulientur suspensi* – 'St Margaret where the hanged men are buried' – as several burials of people with their hands bound together were uncovered. There was a gallows just outside Magdalen Gate, which was within the extra-mural portion of the parish, and the hanged criminals were buried, without any ceremony, in pits in the churchyard.

St Margaret Newbridge Another dedication in honour of Margaret of Antioch, this church stood on the west side of St George's Street, immediately to the north of the bridge, on the site of the Playhouse. It seems to have been one of the last churches to have been founded, and had a small endowment. The Black Death in 1349 effectively depopulated the parish, which was united with St George Colegate. The church was closed and became a hermitage for the hermit who maintained the bridge. It was demolished around 1540.

St Martin-at-Bale The suffix is an anglicisation of Balliva (which is occasionally used), or 'in the bailey', as the church stood within the Castle bailey, although it pre-dated the Castle. St Martin-at-Bale stood approximately across what is now the entrance to Rouen Road from Cattle Market Street. Criminals executed at the Castle and anyone else who died there were buried at St Martin's. The parish had been united with that of

St Michael-at-Thorn for many years, and St Martin's was eventually demolished as surplus to requirements in 1562.

St Mary-in-the-Marsh This was one of the four churches that were enclosed by the Cathedral Close, and the only one left standing once St Ethelbert had been burnt in 1272. It remained until 1564, when the Dean and Chapter, the patrons, decided its upkeep was too great, and closed it. It was gutted, but not demolished, and stood for some time until being turned into dwelling houses. The congregation then worshipped in the south nave aisle of the Cathedral, then in the bishop's chapel, and finally moved to St Luke's chapel. The parish still functions, although it has no church; the font in St Luke's chapel belongs to St Mary's. The site of the church was to the south of the Lower Close, and recent work indicates that much of the building still remains within numbers 10–12, built in 1775, although now internally divided and clad with Georgian brick. A document of 1761 shows the outline of the church, and it seems to have had a chancel and nave, a south porch, a south transept and round west tower.

St Mary Unbrent The suffix means 'unburnt', and if so this may refer to the sacking of the town in 1004 by Sweyn Forkbeard. This church, which stood in Magdalen Street, would have been in the area affected. It may mean that the church was unburnt, as it was of stone, or possibly, as with St Margaret Combust, simply that it was *in combusto*, in the burnt area. The exact site is on the west side of Magdalen Street, and on the south of Golden Dog Lane, which preserves the line of the churchyard path. It was closed and demolished in 1546, and the parish united with St Saviour. It may be possible to trace the outline of the churchyard, if not of the church, from the property boundaries nearby.

St Matthew-at-Palace The church stood in what is now Queen Elizabeth Close, just outside the Cathedral Close wall. The parish was depopulated by the Black Death in 1349, and the church was closed and demolished in 1377. The parish was united with St Martin-at-Palace.

St Michael Conesford The church stood on the east side of King Street, just north of Dragon Hall. It was subsumed into the Austin Friars' precinct in 1290, and they closed and demolished the church in 1360, in order to build a cloister. It seems to have remained in parochial use until then; after that it was united with St Peter Parmentergate.

St Michael Tombland This was effectively the 'civic' church of Anglo-Saxon Norwich. It stood in the middle of Tombland, the main marketplace, with the palace of the Earls of East Anglia to the south and the town house of the Bishops of East Anglia to the north (the seat of the bishopric was not moved to Norwich until 1094). The site is now occupied by the public lavatories, although the green plaque implies it was a little further east. It seems to have been deliberately demolished by the Normans in 1094 simply because it was the principal church. It is unclear what happened to its parish.

St Olave 'Olave' is an anglicisation of Olaf, and refers to the king of Norway, 1016–29, who was responsible for introducing Christianity to Norway. He was killed in battle in 1030, which implies a very late date for the foundation of this church, unless it was an earlier church that was rededicated. It also implies that the parish had a population of Scandinavian origin. The church stood on the corner of Pitt Street and Cherry Lane: the site is mostly now under the roundabout. It was closed in 1534, and demolished three years later; the parish was united with St George Colegate.

St Vedast This is another 'ethnic' dedication, in full to Saints Vaast and Amand. Vaast or Vedast (or even Foster) was Bishop of Arras, and prepared King Clovis for baptism in 496. He is a popular saint in Belgium, but there were only three dedications in England: this one, St Vedast Foster Lane in London, and at Tathwell in Lincolnshire. Amand, another Flemish saint (584–675), appears to have had no connection with Vedast, but they have a joint feast, on 6 February. The dedication may imply an early Flemish population, predating the 16th-century 'Strangers', or it may simply be cultic. The church stood on the north side of Rose Lane, close to the junction with St Vedast Street. It was closed and demolished in 1540, and the parish united with St Peter Parmentergate.

Holy Trinity or Christchurch This church was demolished by the Normans in order to build the Cathedral. Its exact site is not known, but may be under the north transept, or possibly under the crossing of the Cathedral church. It is most likely that the Cathedral's dedication in honour of the Trinity is taken from the church it replaced.

Chapels There were also two chapels, both in King Street, that did not have parochial status. St Anne, dedicated in honour of the mother of the Virgin Mary (though the name was only assigned to her as late as the second century) stood by the river at the east end of St Anne (or Staithe) Lane. St Olaf Southgate stood on the east side of King Street, almost opposite St Peter Southgate, and is dedicated in honour of St Olaf. As with St Olave's church, it may indicate Danish interest. Messent says it was demolished by 1345. Messent also lists a chapel of St Barbara, but this was probably the Guildhall chapel.

The 'anonymous' churches One was uncovered to the south of Anglia Television (the old Agricultural Hall) in 1979: it was a small wooden building consisting of nave and chancel, which was demolished when the castle was built in 1067. Its nave measured 8 by 5 metres, and the chancel was 3 metres square, Excavation uncovered some 130 burials. Further burials, at the north end of Crown Road, may suggest a second church, as they are probably too far from the other site to be the same graveyard.

The possible remains of two more churches were discovered during excavations for Castle Mall, between 1987 and 1991. A rectangular, timber-framed building, surrounded by 85 burials, was found about 25 metres north of the Rouen pub (now 'No 12'). A second possible church was found to the north of the site, suggested by a collection of human remains.

It remains unknown whether these churches were merely demolished, or whether they were removed to other sites (if so, St John Timberhill and St Martin-at-Bale would be likely candidates).

Glossary

Advowson The right to appoint a living (*benefice*) in the Church of England

Aisle A wing or part of a church parallel to, and usually divided by pillars from, the main nave, choir or transept

Alley Although 'aisle' is commonly used to describe the gangway between pews, the more correct term is alley

Altar-piece A piece of art placed on the wall behind the altar – see *reredos*. In the 18th century, these took the form of large classical-style screens. Sometimes called an altar-screen

Annunciation When the Archangel Gabriel announced to Mary that she would be the mother of Jesus. See Luke, chapter 1, verse 26

Apse The semicircular or polygonal end of a chancel or chapel

Apsidal In the shape or form of an *apse*

Arch-braced Curved pair of roof braces forming an arch, connecting the wall (or post) below with the *tie beam* above

Ashlar See *freestone*

Aumbry A cupboard. In the Middle Ages, used to store the communion vessels. Since 1900, in some churches used for keeping the reserved sacrament. See *tabernacle*

Baldachin A canopy over the altar, supported on columns

Benefice An ecclesiastical office

Boss An ornamental knob covering the intersection of ribs in a vault or on a ceiling

Box-pew The true *pew*. Surrounded by wooden panelling, and with a lockable door

Box-tomb A chest-style monument. The interior is a hollow cavity, and the body is buried underground

Burgess An inhabitant of a town or city with full municipal rights

Carolingian Art and architecture influenced by Charlemagne (ruled 800–814) and his successors

Chancel The part of the church at the east end, where the altar stands and where the clergy sit

Chantry chapel A chapel in which masses were said for the soul of its founder

Chapel An area of a church with its own altar, originally for the cult of a saint other than the patron saint. May be an extension, or simply screened off with *parcloses*

Choir stalls Seating running east-west in the *chancel* or crossing, where the choir sits

Clerestory Upper storey of the *nave* wall, rising above the aisle roof. Pierced by windows to light the nave

College of priests A group of priests living in common, but not members of a religious order (unlike monks, friars etc)

Course Continuous layer in a wall, e.g. layer of stones

Crossing The area in the centre of a cruciform church, where the east-west and north-south arms cross

Cruciform Cross-shaped, often of a church floor plan

Cupola Rounded dome forming a roof or ceiling

Cusping Pointed projections in window *tracery* or in arches

Dado The lower, solid part of a *screen*

Decalogue The Ten Commandments

Decorated When capitalised, Decorated refers to a style of architecture dating from c. 1290 to c. 1350, characterised by elaborate window tracery and tall columns. Represents the middle of the *Gothic* period

Early English An architectural style dating from c. 1190 to c. 1250, characterised by the earliest use of pointed arches and representing the beginning of the *Gothic* period

Ecclesiological The study of churches. With a capital E,

it refers specifically to the Ecclesiological Society, which in the 19th century had very fixed and highly influential views about how churches should be built and furnished

Fan vault Form of vault made up of halved concave masonry cones decorated with *blind tracery*

Fittings Interior fixtures, such as *pews*

Flèche Slender spire

Flushwork Decorative patterns in different coloured flint flat against the wall, used to decorate the outside of some churches

Font Container used for the consecrated water used in baptism

Four-centred arch A low elliptical or pointed arch

Freestone Stone, usually oolitic limestone or sandstone, which can be 'freely' worked with metal tools. Thin slabs of freestone used as facing are called ashlar

Furnishings Items in the church interior which are movable, such as lecterns, hangings, etc

Gallery Balcony overlooking the main interior space of a building. Usually at the west end of a church, but some occur in the side-aisles. Generally put up in the 16th to 18th centuries, and removed in the late 19th century

Gothic Art, architecture or decoration styles dating from after the Norman period but before the Renaissance

Gothick Art, architecture or decoration in an 18th-century revival version; predates the 19th-century revival of the true Gothic style

Gradine A shelf behind the altar, usually part of the *reredos*, on which the cross and candlesticks stand

Hammerbeams An abbreviated form of *tie beam* construction, where the central section of the tie beam is omitted

High Church Section of the Church of England that emphasises the Catholic tradition, especially in sacraments, rituals and obedience to church authority – see *Oxford Movement*

Incumbent The cleric in charge of a church. May be called rector, vicar or priest-in-charge

Laudian After Archbishop William Laud (1573–1645), who set up High-Church standards for the Church of England

Lierne vault *Vault* characterised by a star-shaped pattern created by the connecting ribs

Light A vertical division of a window

Living The office of rector or vicar of a particular parish. Sometimes called a *benefice*

Long-and-short work A method of forming *quoins* by placing long narrow blocks of stone alternately with thin wide ones. Characteristic of Anglo-Saxon-style masonry

Medieval Dating from the *Middle Ages*

Middle Ages Currently used for the period from about 450 to about 1540. The period before 1066 is called Early Medieval (formerly 'the Dark Ages') and after 1066 it is called High or Late Medieval

Minster church From about the seventh century until about the ninth, a church which served as a centre of administration for a large district. It was staffed by several priests

Misericord Shelf on a carved bracket placed on the underside of a hinged choir-stall seat. Supports an occupant when standing. Often bears interesting carvings

Moot In the Anglo-Saxon period, the meeting of the men of the local area to transact public business

Mullion The upright in a window; divides the window into a number of *lights*

Narthex Entrance area at the west end of the *nave*

Nave The main body of the church, where the congregation sits

Ogee A double S-shaped curve. Used as an arch form in the 14th century. In a nodding ogee the arch itself inclines forwards, out of the plane of the wall

Open work Wood or stone carving which incorporates holes as part of the design

Orientation A church is assumed to have its altar at the east end. Most deviate from true east to some degree north or south

Oxford Movement Religious movement started in 1833 by Anglican clergymen at the University of Oxford, who sought to renew the Church of England by reviving certain Catholic doctrines and rituals

Parapet A raised rim around the edge of a roof

Parchmark Place where the growth of a crop is stunted (by buried remains) because its roots cannot reach water

Parclose A screen that encloses a side-chapel in a church

Parvise Chamber above a church porch

Patron (a) The patron saint of a church; (b) the person or corporation with the right to appoint the *incumbent*

Pediment A triangular or curved head to panelling. In Norwich churches, only found on 18th-century *altar-pieces*

Perpendicular An architectural style dating from *c*. 1350 to *c*. 1530, characterised by *mullions* reaching to the top of windows, and by the development of *fan vaulting*. Represents the last part of the *Gothic* period

Pews Seating for the laity outside the chancel. What are usually called 'pews' are in fact benches

Pinnacles Projecting points at the corners of a tower, or along a parapet, or topping off a buttress

Piscina Recess in the wall near an altar, with a drain, for washing the communion vessels

Polychrome The use of different colours in various materials for decorative purposes

Pulpit A structure for the priest to speak from, raised above the congregation

Quoins Stones forming the external angles of a wall

Rafter One of the main pieces of timber used in roof construction

Reading-pew or **-desk** A seat with a desk from which the service is read, usually in the *nave*

Reordering When a church has a major interior 'makeover', and the fixtures and fittings are moved or replaced

Reredos A screen or decoration behind the *altar* in a church, usually containing religious images. Often painted wood, but may be carved, gilded etc. Sometimes a tapestry or other fabric is used

Reservation of the sacrament The consecrated elements (bread and wine) are kept in a secure place, usually a cupboard in the wall (*aumbry*) or a box on the altar (*tabernacle*), so that they are available at any time of day or night

Respond A half-pillar attached to a wall, supporting an arch

Reticulated tracery *Tracery* composed of *ogee* arches

Rib vault *Vault* supported by transverse arches springing from the walls

Ritualism The adoption of Catholic practices and forms of worship in church services in the 19th century, associated with the *High Church* movement

Romanesque The architecture of the Anglo-Saxon and Norman styles, *c*. 600–*c*. 1100

Rood The crucifix at the entrance to the chancel. Usually stood on a beam, with attendant figures of St Mary and St John. Some modern versions are suspended, especially where there is no screen

Rood loft A gallery at the top of the *rood screen*, used for access to the lamps burning before the *rood*. Sometimes used for parts of the liturgy

Rood screen A screen dividing the *nave* from the *chancel*, topped with a *rood*

Rood stair A stair for access to the *rood loft*

Sacraments The late medieval church recognised seven: Baptism, Confirmation, Matrimony, Eucharist (Mass), Ordination, Penance (Confession), Extreme Unction ('Last Rites'). The post-Reformation Church of England recognised two: Baptism and Eucharist

Scissor-beamed A form of roof in which the supporting *rafters* cross each other, like a pair of scissors

Sedilia A set of one to three recesses in the chancel wall, used as seats for the clergy during mass

Seven Sacrament font A font which has the seven *sacraments* depicted on the sides of its bowl

Spandrel the space between an arch and its surround. In a roof, the space between a *brace* and a *rafter*

Squint Hole in a wall, usually to allow sight of the altar

Star vault A *vault* with a rib pattern suggesting a star

String course Horizontal *course* or moulding projecting from the surface of a wall

Tabernacle A box to hold the reserved sacrament, which stands on the altar. See *aumbry*

Three-decker pulpit A structure combining a pulpit, a reading-pew and the clerk's desk

Tester Horizontal canopy above an altar or *pulpit*

Thane The lowest rank in the Anglo-Saxon aristocracy

Tie beam A horizontal beam connected to the feet of rafters to prevent them from spreading out under the weight of the roof

Tierceron A *rib vault* with subsidiary (tierceron) ribs

Tracery Openwork pattern of masonry or wood in the upper part of an opening, e.g window or screen: blind tracery is applied to a solid wall; Y-tracery has *mullions* branching into a Y shape

Transept Part of a church built at right-angles to the main structure. May be added to an existing church, or be part of a *cruciform* building

Tree of Jesse Based on Isaiah chapter 11, verses 1–3: "A shoot shall come from the stump of Jesse." In art, Jesse, the father of King David, is shown reclining, with a tree growing from his loins. The branches are labelled with the names of the various ancestors of Jesus, showing that he was indeed descended from David

Trefoil An ornamental device with three lobes

Truss Supporting structure or framework

Tympanum A vertical triangular space forming the centre of a *pediment*

Vault An arched stone roof; a burial chamber

Zigzag course *Course* with abrupt alternate right and left turns

A useful source for further reference is *A Companion to the English Parish Church* by Stephen Friar (Sutton Publishing, new edition 1998).

Bibliography

Ayers, B *Norwich: Archaeology of a Fine City*, Stroud 2009
Barringer, C (ed) *Norwich in the Nineteenth Century*, Norwich 1984
Cambridge, E 'The architecture of the Augustinian mission' in Gameson, R (ed), *St Augustine and the Conversion of England*, Stroud 1999
Friars, S *A Companion to the English Parish Church*, Stroud 1998
Gilchrist, R *Norwich Cathedral Close: the evolution of the English cathedral landscape*, Woodbridge 2005
Meeres, F *A History of Norwich*, Chichester 1998
Messent, CJW *The City Churches of Norwich*, Norwich 1932
Pevsner, N (revised Wilson, B) *The Buildings of England: (Norfolk 1: Norwich and North-east)*, London 1997
Plunkett, G *Disappearing Norwich*, Lavenham 1987
Plunkett, G *Rambles in Old Norwich*, Lavenham 1990
Rawcliffe, C and Wilson, R (eds) *Medieval Norwich*, London 2004
Rawcliffe, C and Wilson, R (eds) *Norwich since 1550*, London 2004
Sillett, J *Views of the Churches, Chapels, and other Public Edifices in the City of Norwich*, Norwich 1828
Spencer, N and Kent, A *The Old Churches of Norwich*, Norwich 1970 (revised edition 1990
Taylor, HM and Taylor, J *Anglo-Saxon Architecture*, Cambridge 1965

Individual churches
Most of the churches have produced guidebooks or leaflets over the years, many of which have been ephemeral; those listed here are only the more substantial productions:

Anon *St Stephen's Church, Norwich: a visitor's guide*, Norwich (no date)
Beazley, O and Ayers, B 'Two Medieval Churches in Norfolk: St Martin-at-Palace and St Michael, Bowthorpe' *East Anglian Archaeology Reports* no 96, 2001
Coiley, DEM *The Church of St George Tombland, Norwich*, Norwich 1974
Duxson, WE *Maddermarket*, Norwich 1931
Eade, P *Some Account of the Parish of St Giles, Norwich*, Norwich 1886
Flood, RH *A Description of St Julian's Church, Norwich, and an account of Dame Julian's connection with it*, Norwich (no date)
Groves, NW *Saint George Tombland, Norwich, a guide to the church and its furniture*, Norwich 1996 (2nd edition 2007; 3rd edition 2009)
Groves, NW T*he Church of St Michael-at-Plea, Norwich: some aspects of its history*, Norwich 2009
Hale, R *The Churches of King Street, Norwich, in medieval and Victorian times*, Norwich 1999
Hubbard, LA *The Church of St George Colegate in Norwich over the water*, Norwich (no date)
Jessopp, J *History and Antiquities of St Gregory's Church, Norwich*, Norwich 1886
Kent, EA *The Church of St Peter Hungate, Norwich*, Norwich (no date, c1930)
McLaren, S *St Augustine's Church, Norwich*, London 2004
McLean, MS *St Julian's Church and Lady Julian's Cell*, Norwich 1979/1981
McLean, MS and Upjohn S *A Guide to St John Timberhill*, Norwich 1982 (revised Mountney, JM, 1989)
Pennell, TEN *The Annals of the Church of St Michael and All Angels, Coslany, Norwich*, Norwich 1925
Raymond L *The Church of St John the Baptist, Maddermarket, Norwich*, London 1993
Tillett, EA *St George Tombland: past and present*, Norwich 1891
Tricker, R *All Saints Church, Norwich: history and guide*, Norwich 1982; 2nd edition 1992; 3rd edition 2004
Tricker, R *The Church of St John the Baptist, Maddermarket*, London 2001

Manuscript sources, held in the Norfolk Heritage Centre:
Tillett, EA 'Norwich Scrapbooks': usually one volume for each parish (42 volumes; nos. 2, 4, and 6 were destroyed in the 1994 fire) N942.615
Postcard collection; Norwich churches under NE

Held at the Norfolk Record Office:
Each parish's documents are to be found within the sequence PD.
MC 445: MS church notes by Noel Spencer
MC 1619/1: Thomas Lord's notes on services in all the churches and chapels of Norwich, 1884

Acknowledgements

Nicholas Groves I am grateful to a number of people who have wittingly (or, indeed, otherwise) helped in shaping this book.

First are those who have examined, argued over and generally appreciated the churches with me over many years: Terry Adkin, Brian Ayers, Peter Brice, Charles Carus, Jon Crampton, Jon Finch, Roberta Gilchrist, Paul Greener, Michael Mountney, Rory Quinn, Gerald Randall, Kate Smith, Owen Thompson, Kate Weaver, Clive Wilkins-Jones and Michael Wingate, as well as colleagues at the Norwich Historic Churches Trust, and many groups of students.

Second, I would like to thank those clergy and others who have custody of the buildings, and who have made access easy, and found time to discuss them.

More formal thanks go to those whose own publications I have used. I did not think that a work of this nature needed footnotes, but the bibliography contains the printed sources I have used over the years. It also indicates the manuscript sources, most of which are in the Norfolk Record Office. Finally, thanks to the staff of the Norfolk Record Office and the Norfolk Heritage Centre for assisting in my research.

I am also very grateful to Norwich HEART for agreeing to publish the book: Michael Loveday, the chief executive; Sophie Cabot; and especially Christina Lister, who oversaw the publication. Charlie Watson and his colleagues at East Publishing have ensured a good end product.

I owe an especial debt to the late Nigel Yates of the University of Wales, Lampeter, for his stimulating and encouraging supervision of my own research into the churches of the later 19th century. It is a matter of great sadness to me that his untimely death has prevented us visiting them together.

Christina Lister and Michael Loveday, HEART We would like to acknowledge the countless organisations and dedicated staff and volunteers who work tirelessly to support, protect and promote Norwich's medieval churches all year, every year.

For this book there are a few special thanks and acknowledgements we would like to make. Firstly, to Nick Groves, who has written a comprehensive and authoritative text on Norwich's set of medieval churches which we hope people will enjoy and be inspired by for years to come. Secondly, to Rachel Codling, and to Anthony Denny, Mike Jefferies, Andrew Johnson, Bernie Sheehan, Charlotte Stratta and Charlie Watson at East Publishing for believing in the project and creating another beautiful and original book with us.

We would also like to thank the following people for being interviewed for the book, providing fascinating insights and personal reflections on elements of our medieval churches: Anne Allen, Brian Ayers, Louise Bohn, the Reverend Jack Burton, Sophie Cabot, Peter Callan, Ellen Clarke, Lucy Conroy, Dale Copley, Julia de Salis, Kate Egglestone, Steve Foyster, Rosemary Frost, Katherine Gray, Loyd Grossman, the Reverend Canon Jeremy Haselock, David Helsdon, Fred Higginson, the Reverend Madeline Light, Canon Michael McLean, Barry Ross, Brian Sargent, Cora Shearing, Father Martin Smith, Owen Thompson, Michael Wingate, Rosamunde Woods, Ian Woods, Dr William Woods and a Great Hospital resident who wished to remain anonymous.

And finally we would like to thank the following organisations and people for kindly letting us use their photography to illustrate the book: Norfolk Library and Information Service, Norfolk Museums & Archaeology Service (Norwich Castle Museum & Art Gallery), Norwich Arts Centre, Ricky-Joe Burrage, Mike Dixon, Ian 'Harry' Harris, Simon Knott, David Plummer, George and Jonathan Plunkett, Leo Reynolds, Marion Ridgley, John Sapey, 'Seany 1968', Cameron Self, Chris Skipworth, Richard Tilbrook, EM Trendell, Roy Tricker and Emma Whitcombe.

Photographers who submitted images to the 2009 Norwich HEART photography competition on Norwich's medieval churches: Jan Barsby, Joan Blazeby, Julia Cameron, Ian Coldicott, David Drinkwater, David Edleston, Raymond Gouldsmith, George Ishmael, Helen Litterick, Tracy Martin, Sheena McIntyre-Warnock, Gary Rayner, David Sherwood, Jeffrey Taylor, Paul Venn and David White.

Index

All Saints Fyebriggate*143, 145
All Saints Centre 16, 17
All Saints, Westlegate 14–17, 57, 72, 123, 145
Anglo-Catholic 67, 85, 120
Anglo-Saxon 11, 23, 26, 30, 61, 65, 72, 88, 90, 92, 105, 134
Anglo-Saxon Chronicle 30
Anguish, Thomas 42, 43
Anne of Bohemia 52
Antell, John 19, 85, 101
Appleyard, William 19
Assembly House 97, 113

Bacon, Francis 50
Berney, Richard 118, 120, 121
Bishop's Palace 90
Black Death 12, 75, 146
Blomefeld, Francis 26, 108, 145
Boardman, Edward 20, 32, 34
Bridewell Museum 19
Brooke Report 12, 13
Browne, Sir Thomas 115

Caen stone 92
Castle Mall 147
Catholic Apostolic Church 97
Chapelfield 132
Christchurch – *see Holy Trinity*
Christchurch New Catton 13, 28
Church of the New Jerusalem 97
Churches Conservation Trust, The 9, 12, 13, 24, 25, 62, 79
College of St Mary-in-the-Field 11, 97, 108, 113
Colton, John 47
Community of All Hallows 57
Comper, Ninian 113
Crome, John 37, 38

Dame Julian 72, 74, 75
de Guader, Ralph, Earl of Norfolk 114
Decorated 12, 15, 26, 32, 35, 46, 49, 52, 80, 85, 92, 97, 102
Domesday Book 61, 88
Duke's Palace 61
Dutch and Flemish Studies Centre 98

Ecclesiological Society 12
Elizabeth I, Queen 28, 61
England, George Pike 21, 37

Father Ignatius 79
French Borough 44
French Church – *see St Mary-the-Less*
Friends of Norwich Churches 124
Georgian 13, 40
Glover, Sarah 6, 77, 78
'Great Blow' of 1648 131
Green, Thomas 50
Great Hospital 11, 12, 52
Gurney, John Joseph 71

Hansard, Luke 92, 94
HEART – *see Norwich Heritage Economic & Regeneration Trust*
Heritage Open Days 10, 20, 35, 82, 124, 156
High Church 40, 57, 71
Holy Trinity or Christchurch* 11, 12, 147
Hospital of St Giles – *see Great Hospital*
Hungate Medieval Art 9, 108, 110, 111

Irvingites – *see Catholic Apostolic Church*
Ivory, Thomas 50, 52

Jannys, Robert 37, 38

Kemp, William 61, 62
Kett's Rebellion 28
King of Norwich 50, 61, 72
King, Michael 80

Low Countries 98

Morris, William 42, 88

Nelson, Horatio 21, 134
NHCT – *see Norwich Historic Churches Trust*
Norfolk Archaeological Trust 110
Norfolk Association for the Care and Resettlement of Offenders (Norfolk ACRO) 90
Norman 32, 34, 90, 91, 92, 121
Norwich Arts Centre 134, 137
Norwich Castle 12, 146

Norwich Castle Museum & Art Gallery 50
Norwich Cathedral 12, 40, 49, 52, 85, 105, 115, 126, 146, 147
Norwich Centre for Martial Arts 120, 121
Norwich Christian Resource Centre 106
Norwich City Corporation 52
Norwich City Council 13
Norwich Heritage Economic & Regeneration Trust (HEART) 9, 10
Norwich Historic Churches Trust (NHCT) 6, 7, 9, 10, 12, 13, 16, 28, 30, 105, 110, 111, 124
Norwich Over-the-Water 13
Norwich Puppet Theatre 57, 58
Norwich School of Artists 37, 50
Norwich School, The 121
Norwich shawls 16
Norwich Society, The 126

Oberammergau 65, 72
Octagon Chapel 10, 145
Old Meeting House Congregational Church 10, 110
Onoak Studios 87
Oxford Movement 34, 71, 82, 108

Parish of Parmentergate 13, 16, 35
Paston family 108
Peasants' Revolt 75
Perpendicular 12, 15, 26, 30, 32, 37, 40, 46, 49, 57, 69, 85, 92, 97, 102, 108, 118, 123
Pettus family 126, 129
Pevsner, Nikolaus 23, 94, 113
Phipson, RM 23, 46, 131
Pre-Raphaelite 61

Reformation 7, 12, 30, 50, 69, 97, 98, 131
Renaissance 121, 131
Revelations of Divine Love 74, 75
Richard II, King 52

Ritualism 6, 28, 50, 61, 77, 79, 142
Roman Catholic Cathedral of St John 12
Romanesque 11, 12, 74

Scott, John Oldrid 70, 71
Singleton, Robert 50
St Andrew 13, 18–21, 40, 42, 140, 145
St Anne (chapel)* 147
St Augustine 12, 13, 22–25, 94
St Bartholomew* 10, 139
St Benedict* 10, 13, 21, 92, 140
St Botolph* 145
St Catherine Newgate* 145
St Christopher*145
St Clement-at-Fyebridge 13, 26–29, 145
St Clement-at-the-Well* 145
St Clement Conesford – *see St Clement-at-the-Well*
St Crowches* 10, 141
St Cuthbert*145
St Edmund 30–31
St Edward the Martyr* 145
St Ethelbert*12, 145
St Etheldreda 12, 32–35, 92, 144, 145
St Etheldreda Artist Studio 35
St Francis Heartsease 35
St George Colegate 12, 13, 24, 36–39, 40, 123, 145, 146, 147
St George Tombland 6, 11, 13, 16, 21, 30, 40–43, 97, 110, 126
St Giles-on-the-Hill 11, 13, 44–47, 79, 102
St Gregory, Pottergate 13, 46, 48–51, 77, 102
St Gregory's Centre for Arts 51
St Helen, Bishopgate 11, 12, 52–55
St James, Pockthorpe 56–59
St John Colegate*12, 145
St John Maddermarket 12, 13, 60–63, 102, 113
St John the Evangelist*12, 121, 145
St John Timberhill 10, 12, 13, 15, 16, 64–67, 142, 147
St John-de-Sepulchre 12, 13, 68–71, 139

St Julian
6, 9, 12, 13, 15, 16, 57,
72–75, 92, 142,145
St Lawrence 13, 21, 76–79
St Luke Aylsham Road
13,24
St Margaret Combust
80,146
St Margaret-de-Westwick
13,51,80–83,146
St Margaret Fybriggate –
see St Margaret Combust
St Margaret
Newbridge*12, 80, 146
St Martin-at-Bale* 146,
147
St Martin-at-Oak 37, 84–
87
St Martin-at-Palace 13,
88–91, 146
St Mary Coslany 24, 92–
95, 97, 101
St Mary Unbrent* 97, 146
St Mary's College – see
College of St Mary-in-
the-Field
St Mary-in-the-Marsh*
97, 146
St Mary-the-Great – see
College of St Mary-in-
the-Field
St Mary-the-Less 96–99,
145
St Mary Magdalen Silver
Road 57
St Matthew-at-Palace* 12,
146
St Michael
Conesford*12,121,147
St Michael Coslany (St
Miles) 46, 50, 61, 100–
103
St Michael Motstow – see
St Michael-at-Plea
St Michael Tombland* 147
St Michael-at-Plea
21, 42, 104–107
St Michael-at-Thorn*
10, 13, 72, 142, 146
St Michael-super-Montem
– see St Michael-at-Thorn
St Miles – see St Michael
Coslany
St Miles-on-the-Hill – see
St Michael-at-Thorn
St Olaf Southgate* (chapel)
147
St Olave* 147
St Paul* 10, 92, 143, 146
St Peter Hungate
9, 13, 42, 92, 108–111

St Peter Mancroft
13, 21, 44, 46, 61, 112–
117, 140
St Peter Parmentergate
13, 118–121, 146, 147
St Peter Southgate*
10, 12, 34, 144, 147
St Saviour 15, 37, 122–
125, 141, 146
St Simon and St Jude
12, 13, 126–129
St Stephen 13, 44, 46,
130–133
St Swithin 13, 134–137
St Vedast*121, 147
Strangers 97, 98, 147
Suckling, Sir John 21
Swedenborgians –
see Church of the
New Jerusalem

Travers, Martin 66, 67
Trinity URC 102

United Benefice of St
George Tombland 13
United Benefice of St Giles
13

Walloon Church 97
World War I 23, 50
World War II 10, 12, 72,
92, 138, 140

*lost churches

1 All Saints, Westlegate E3
2 St Andrew D3
3 St Augustine, Gildencroft B2
4 St Clement-at-Fyebridge C3
5 St Edmund, Fishergate B4
6 St Etheldreda, King Street F5
7 St George Colegate C3
8 St George Tombland C4
9 St Giles-on-the-Hill D1
10 St Gregory, Pottergate D2
11 St Helen, Bishopgate C5
12 St James, Pockthorpe B4
13 St John Maddermarket D3
14 St John Timberhill E3
15 St John-de-Sepulchre G4
16 St Julian, King Street F4
17 St Lawrence D2
18 St Margaret-de-Westwick C2
19 St Martin-at-Oak B2
20 St Martin-at-Palace B4
21 St Mary Coslany B2
22 St Mary-the-Less (French Church) D4
23 St Michael Coslany (St Miles) C2
24 St Michael-at-Plea D4
25 St Peter Hungate C4
26 St Peter Mancroft E2
27 St Peter Parmentergate E4
28 St Saviour B3
29 St Simon and St Jude C4
30 St Stephen E3
31 St Swithin C1

Lost churches

32 All Saints Fyebriggate A3
33 St Bartholomew, Ber Street (demolished 1549) F4
34 St Benedict (bombed, 1942) C1
35 St Botolph B3
36 St Catherine Newgate G3
37 St Christopher D3
38 St Clement-at-the-Well F5
39 St Crowches (demolished 1551) D3
40 St Cuthbert D4
41 St Edward the Martyr G5
42 St Ethelbert D4
43 St John Colegate C3
44 St John the Evangelist D4
45 St Margaret Combust A3
46 St Margaret Newbridge C3
47 St Martin-at-Bale E4
48 St Mary-in-the-Marsh D5
49 St Mary Unbrent B3
50 St Matthew-at-Palace C5
51 St Michael Conesford E4
52 St Michael-at-Thorn (bombed, 1942) F4
53 St Michael Tombland D4
54 St Olave B3
55 St Paul (bombed, 1942) B4
56 St Peter Southgate (demolished 1887) G5
57 St Vedast D5
58 Holy Trinity or Christchurch C4
59 Chapels (St Ann E5, St Olaf Southgate G5)
60 The 'anonymous' churches D4/E4

Accessibility

Accessibility to the churches varies and is subject to change, so it is recommended you check the latest opening times and accessibility information for each church before visiting. Visit the Norwich Historic Churches Trust's website (www.norwich-churches.org) or contact Norwich Tourist Information Centre: 01603 213999, tourism@norfolk.gov.uk for more information.

The whole set of churches is usually open for the Heritage Open Days event every September, coordinated by HEART. For more information visit www.heritagecity.org or call 01603 305575.

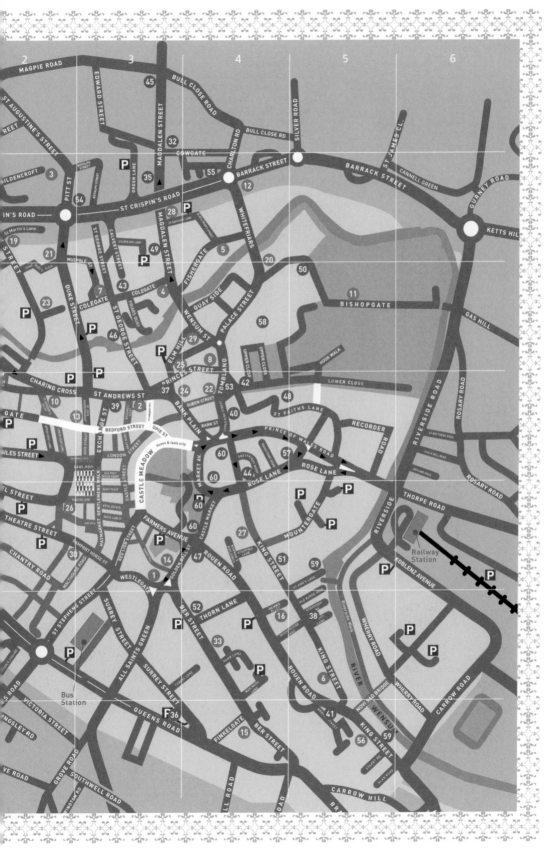